The Mindful Parent

The Mindful Parent

HOW TO STAY SANE, STAY CALM AND STAY CONNECTED TO YOUR KIDS

SHIRLEY PASTIROFF

Renew Your Mind

— PUBLISHING —

First published 2020
Renew Your Mind Publishing
www.renewyourmind.co.nz

ISBN 9780473520168

A catalogue record for this book is available from the National Library of New Zealand

Note

The author would like to acknowledge the work of Chantal Hofstee, Gordon Neufeld, Pauline Skeates and Byron Katie.

Some of the material in this book was published in the books Mindfulness on the Run and Renew Your Mind by author Chantal Hofstee and is used in this book in an updated and adapted manner with permission from the author.

Designed and Illustrated by Husk

Disclaimer

This book is a general guide only and should never be a substitute for the skill, knowledge and experience of a qualified medical professional dealing with facts, circumstances and symptoms of a particular case. The medical and health information presented in this book on the research, training and professional experience of the author, and is true and complete to the best of their knowledge. However, this book is intended only as an informative guide; it is not intended to replace or countermand the advice given by the reader's personal physician. Because each person and situation is unique, the author and the publisher urge the reader to check with a qualified healthcare professional before using any procedure where there is a question as to its appropriateness. The author, publisher and their distributors are not responsible for any adverse effects or consequences resulting from the use of the information in this book. It is the responsibility of the reader to consult a physician or other qualified healthcare professional regarding their personal care. The intent of the information provided is to be helpful; however, there is no guarantee of results associated with the information provided.

"This is one of those rare books which takes an incredibly complex but hugely important subject and turns that into simple tools we can all understand and apply. If you sometimes struggle to be the kind of parent you want to be... this book is an absolute must."

~ *Nigel Latta, clinical psychologist, author & speaker + dad of 2.*

"In 20+ years of parenting programmes and resources none have impacted our family more than Shirley's Mindful Parenting. From frustration to connection; from red brain to green brain; Shirley has taught us – simply but profoundly – how to have the kind of relationship with our children we all dream of. I'm SO excited she's now put that material into a book!"

~ *Greg Fleming, CEO Parenting Place + dad of 5*

"Parenting can be the best of times and the worst of times, Mindful Parenting has changed the emotional fabric of our home, there is now more peace and at the same time more effective action! The tools in this book helped me trust in myself more and support my children to process their difficult emotions and come out the other side able to think and act in healthy ways. I'm pleased to report there is less losing of my s#*t."

~ *Petra Bagust, broadcaster & communicator + mum of 3*

"I am frequently asked how on earth we can raise resilient and happy children in the over-scheduled and busy world we live in today. The answer is Mindful Parenting. Here, Shirley Pastiroff, outlines simple and effective practices that are loaded with meaning and power and serve to achieve exactly that - happy and resilient relationships. Her practical and down to earth style makes this easily achievable for parents."

~ *Nathan Wallis, neuroscience educator + dad of 3*

"With the explosion of social media and the ubiquitous digital world our children operate in, the need for connection with our kids is more important now than ever. Mindful Parenting is a refreshing and timely book that's a must for all parents – offering insightful and tangible steps to help navigate our relationships and truly connect with our children."

~ Nikki Denholm, director The Light Project + mum of 3

"As a surgeon and father of five, I found Shirley's book a compelling read. It anchors the latest insights from neuroscience with actionable, practical, and surprisingly simple ways to be the parent you want to be. If you're interested in understanding your innate responses to the challenges of parenting, creating a calmer and healthier connection with your children, and experiencing less parental guilt as a result, this book truly delivers".

~ Zac Moaveni, paediatric surgeon + dad of 5

"For a long time I felt helpless during those trying moments with the kids, but with the practical approach Shirley offers in The Mindful Parent I feel empowered with the tools to help navigate those tricky times while still maintaining a deep connection with my kids. This approach is helping me be the father I want to be".

~ Ido Drent, actor + dad of 2.

To Frankie, Jonah, Evie, Roxy and Lily
For introducing me to a much better life

Contents

Introduction   11

Chapter 1   What colour is your brain?   19

Chapter 2   Mindfulness really matters   47

Chapter 3   Emotions are your friends   71

Chapter 4   Connection - The magic ingredient   103

Chapter 5   Resolving conflict without losing your sh*t   145

Chapter 6   Thoughts become things   197

Chapter 7   Growing your mindful family   217

Introduction

It was a Thursday morning and I was at the shops buying a lunchbox for one of my five kids to – yet again – replace the one she'd lost. I spent a bit of extra time choosing one I knew she'd love, rather than grabbing something plain and cheap, which is what I felt she deserved given her carelessness. I was feeling a little bit saintly as it sat on the kitchen bench waiting for her to come home and love it and be really grateful.

On Thursday afternoon she screwed up her nose at my choice. I threw the lunchbox across the kitchen and it didn't survive the impact. By Thursday evening it was in the bin. I didn't just throw the lunchbox, I shouted and I swore – just to round out the scene for you. My 7-year-old wisely hid under the sofa cushions until it was safe to come out while my 9-year old sent me upstairs to calm down, "like you tell us to Mummy". While I was cooling off, I had two trains of thought.

The first went like this:

She's lost TWO lunchboxes in THREE days; I've spent hours of my life at the shops buying stuff for my kids, who all seem to like losing things as much as I hate shopping. I even chose that lunchbox carefully thinking she'd love it. How dare she get upset with me for getting the wrong one?

This is the 'list-of-justifications' recovery method.

My second train of thought went more like this:

No... no... no... no! Why couldn't I have stopped myself from throwing it? And stopped the words coming out of my mouth? Do they get over this stuff? Does it scar them for life? None of my friends parent this badly. And now I've got another lunchbox to buy.

This is the 'all-my-fault' recovery method.

Two reactions - both of them as unhelpful as each other: the reasons my children were utterly to blame, and the reasons why I should have known better. Both regular conversations in my head, and both creating their own impossible feedback loop. No parent glides back into family life with love and presence while this stuff is turning circles in their brain. And I definitely didn't. On numerous occasions, it was only a matter of time before a tantrum, a scuffle, a spilt drink, a screen-time row, or just an unpopular dinner drove me back upstairs to lick my wounds and rage about their shortcomings, followed swiftly by beating myself up about my own. And so, despite our family looking pretty passable in public, behind the scenes chaos and unpredictability became our norm.

THE BACKGROUND

My journey into parenting had actually started off quite well, with a first baby who ate and slept according to the manual. So we had another. With two very close together and an international move, life became more challenging. I remember getting dressed one morning in our new rental home, and wondering if my one and two-year-old could manage by themselves for a few years, or if I could loan them out for a while to someone else who knew what they were doing.

Deep down I thought I probably was the best person for the job, but because I was having as many meltdowns as they were, I was pretty sure I wasn't doing my job very well.

Our lives settled down and we had one more child. It was a challenge but we were doing ok. My partner is calm, so the kids had a great dad, and I constantly tried to overlook the fact that I couldn't keep my cool in quite the same way. I told myself that it was because I was at home with them all day and saw them more, so it made sense that I was a little more volatile.

Two years later we had a beautiful and double surprise: identical twins. The stakes shot up. Our eldest was just six, our next one not yet in school, and our third was still in nappies. This time the wheels really started to come off.

We still had many great days. I was a great parent when they were great kids. A simple equation; when they behaved, I behaved. When they didn't, I didn't. With five children, the windows of opportunity when all of them were 'behaving' declined sharply. It took only one child being challenging for me to feel anxious. Two was generally enough to tip me into stress. Three or more and we deteriorated into chaos.

There were lots of days that I promised myself for the thousandth time that I would never yell at them like that again. I would see that face of fear looking back at me, and know I'd gone too far, and wish I could take back those last few minutes. Then I'd do it all over again. Some of you know what I mean I'm sure.

And so my children lived in this strange and slightly unsafe world. I gave them lots of love and attention, but if I couldn't handle them I would get angry and emotional or I'd withdraw from them.

Almost all of my chaotic reactions were in private. In public I was quite impressive. There's nothing like leaving the house with five children who look mostly clean and happy, to get lots of compliments. I think it's one of the reasons I love other parents so much. The mums – and it was mostly mums that I hung out with – were so generous, so quick to let me know they thought I was amazing, and how did I do it?

Even though I heard the nervous "I can't even manage two" murmured following my reply, I enjoyed the attention. *If only they knew* hovered just beneath the surface for me, but my kids seemed to be doing well so I wondered if parenting was just a rollercoaster and what I was experiencing was normal.

However, I could also see similarities to patterns I had grown up with that I didn't like. I wasn't just out of my depth by being so outnumbered,

I could also feel the influence of my own parents who – although they loved me dearly – had found parenting challenging. As a child I remember feeling that I had to be a good girl in order to be sure of their love, and our home became unpredictable when things didn't go according to plan.

I knew my upbringing had influenced patterns of anxiety and self-criticism that I experienced, but I had always been determined to parent differently. I intended to be unconditional in my love. I wanted my children to feel fully accepted. And I planned to offer my kids a home full of fun and laughter, warmth and connection.

These were great ideas in theory, but I discovered that they were completely impractical. When I was under pressure I could clearly see the same reactive patterns in myself that I'd seen in my home growing up. Unwittingly I was repeating the same message all over again.

I frantically searched for solutions, and tried a few different techniques and approaches I came across that were supposed to help. There were sticker charts and other reward systems, time outs and 'natural' consequences, more quality time with each child, more quality time for me, less sugar for them, less alcohol for me, less screen time for them, and more structured routines for all of us.

Some of them worked for a while but, in the end, when I was triggered by my children's behaviour, it all went downhill. In those moments, I couldn't use any of the approaches kindly and calmly, which apparently was the right way to use them. At one of my lowest points I found myself trying unsuccessfully to take a sticker off my son's sticker chart, as he had apparently 'un-earned' it. For those of you who haven't tried it, it's remarkably hard to do.

During those early years with my family, I also decided to retrain as a counsellor, just to add to my already fraught life. I'd always been fascinated by people – why they think and feel the way they do and how they grow and change. Researching ideas of wellbeing and mental health was a wonderful distraction for me but, looking back, I was also on a journey to understand why I reacted to life the way I did and what would help me, as well as being interested in what would be beneficial for anyone else.

My journey led me to a much wider exploration; to understanding stress in a whole new way. It led me to mindfulness and to empathy. More than anything, it led me to an understanding of, and relationship with, my brain for the first time in my life. The missing pieces of the puzzle started to fall into place and both my life and my parenting began to change.

I'm a few years on now, and it's been an extraordinary journey for me to go from trying to hide how chaotic our home really was, to working with thousands of parents and teaching a new style of parenting. However, it's not all new. My approach is based on ancient ideas of how relationships work, how children thrive, and how parents and children relate naturally, all embedded in contemporary brain science.

This book is about how those changes have happened in the homes and lives of so many parents I've worked with, as well as in my own. It will enable you to make powerful shifts in your life – changes that will help you connect deeply with your children and move through your family life with more presence and more joy. It's not a book that will add more to your endless to-do list but will point you back towards your deepest intuition. It will bring you back to yourself, simplify parenting down to its core, bring more calm to your home on even the most chaotic days, and help you to create deeper and more lasting connections with your children.

I still yell and I still have meltdowns. There are days that remind me of how it used to be. I still throw the occasional lunchbox, trot out the odd four-letter bomb, or give up in despair at being the worst parent in the world. But those days are few and far between and my recovery is quick.

Now there is more fun and more freedom – for me and for my kids. I know how my brain works, how my thoughts work for me and against me, and what role my emotions play in my reactions. I also have tools and techniques that are so kind and effective it's hard not to use them. And that leaves me free to love my children and connect with them in ways I never thought were possible.

There are no parenting experts; don't be fooled. I am not one. However, I have stories to tell of how transformation is possible in our lives, and techniques to share that enable that to happen. And the result is that we get to launch our children into the world with firmer roots and stronger wings, and not lose our own lives while doing it.

The focus of The Mindful Parent is us rather than our children. My children are a little different – they are more resilient than they were, they bounce back from disappointment more quickly and they have more emotional awareness. But the biggest difference has been in me. I feel as if I have a protective cushion around me, like having suspension with decent shock-absorbers. Life with children, especially with five, is no less 'shocking' or bumpy than it's always been, but I don't feel it as acutely, I react much less strongly, and we have so much more fun.

So I've written this book for anyone who is finding parenting hard, but changing your children even harder.

So we start with us.

HOW TO USE THIS BOOK

The Mindful Parent invites you on a journey that has the potential to change your brain and transform your home. It's not a book of information as much as an invitation to new experiences, which require a little self-examination and a few short but regular practices or exercises.

In each chapter there's theory, research, stories, simple techniques and questions to help you discover more about yourself.

All the practices in this book I use on a regular basis and they're designed with the idea of subtraction rather than addition, in mind. We don't need to add more to our lives, to work harder or become more skilful as parents – it's really the complete opposite. Instead, we need to rediscover that parenting is actually the most natural thing in the world, and, ironically, that takes a little practice.

Read through cover to cover before circling back, or do the exercises as you go along – whatever feels right for you. Put the material to the test in your own life.

My hope is that you will find yourself returning to your deepest intuition about how your children thrive and how you might offer them the best environment to do just that, as well as discovering with confidence that you are the perfect parent for them.

1. What colour is your brain?

"Rabbit's clever," said Pooh thoughtfully.
"Yes," said Piglet, "Rabbit's clever."
"And he has Brain."
"Yes," said Piglet, "Rabbit has Brain."
There was a long silence.
"I suppose," said Pooh, "that that's why he never understands anything."

~ A.A. Milne

In each of us there is another whom we do not know.

~ Carl Jung

It turns out that our brain is the best place to start when we want to understand, and then change, anything that's not quite working the way we'd like it to in our lives. It's definitely not where I expected to start, having avoided science as much as I could at school. However, everywhere else that I looked for help on how to become a better parent, or turn my children into better children, or create a happier home, turned into dead ends for me. As I looked further, I also discovered that what scientists now know about the brain is a secret that really shouldn't be kept for those that love lab coats, MRI scans and complicated equations.

For me, it's been a total relief to start somewhere concrete. Parenting is so personal and so emotive, not to mention the fact that the stakes are high – it matters so much. And despite being an apparently natural thing to do, we seem to have lost a lot of our intuition about how to do it. Instead of surrounding ourselves with truly helpful and life-giving information, we often surround ourselves with guilt and comparisons instead.

The intensity with which we want to get parenting right, combined with the fact that our children come in gorgeous and entirely unpredictable technicolour, causes all sorts of problems. We scramble to find tools or techniques that mean we'll have free-spirited, creative little humans who also do what we say and keep their rooms tidy. It's a tricky combination and the parenting world seems to be drowning in all the possible ways we can create the kids we want, whilst producing more stressed-out parents than ever before.

NEUROPLASTICITY: IT'S NEVER TOO LATE TO CHANGE YOUR BRAIN

So what do we know about our brain, and how can it help us here? The human brain is the most complex part of the body – the most complex thing we know of in the universe – and we only know a fraction of what there is to discover about it so far. However, what we do know is important for understanding how we live our lives.

We know that our children's brains are dynamic and develop rapidly as they grow. Until recently though, scientists thought our brains stopped changing as we got to adulthood and became hardwired. 'Neuroplasticity' is the word now used to describe the discovery that our brains are plastic throughout our lives, which means they continue to adapt and create new neural pathways, even into our adult lives. This, in itself, has huge implications.

Neuroplasticity makes sense of how some people recover from brain injuries, how we learn an instrument or a new language, and why although those things may be harder as adults than as children, they are still possible. It's the word now often also used to explain the processes in our brain when we learn new responses and new behaviours, as well as new skills.

The simplest explanation for neuroplasticity is that we have billions of pathways connecting the neurons in our brain, and the ones we use the most regularly become the ones we use most regularly. The most travelled paths turn into our default patterns. This happens at every stage of our lives, but often the basic framework for our brain's responses are laid down when we're very young.

This is good news and bad news depending on our childhood, our personality, and our experiences. Some of us have solid, helpful wiring by the time we become adults. We're wired for self-confidence, optimism and resilience. Others of us didn't get so lucky and find ourselves hitting adulthood with a less helpful network of well-used pathways.

Even when we didn't have a great start, if our adult lives have worked fairly well for us, we may have been able to keep these underlying patterns hidden away. However, parenting is so intense that there's really no place to hide. For me, parenting wasn't altogether a shock, as I had discovered a number of my personal patterns of reactivity long before I had children. However for many people, the first discovery of these patterns – or well-trodden neural pathways – is when children come along. One of the phrases I hear most often from my clients is, "I really wasn't an angry person until I had kids".

When we encounter patterns of reactivity to our children's behaviour, we often try to solve the problem by starting with our children. How can we get them to listen, do what we say, not whine, not be so sensitive, so insensitive, so annoying, so disrespectful? It makes sense to an extent, but this is the hardest place to start.

So much has been taught and written from the starting point of changing our children, but in my experience – both personally and professionally – it doesn't work so well. If you've ever tried to change anyone else, be they a partner or a friend, you'll know how hard it is. Our main responsibility, even as a parent, is our own responses. And it's our own responses that are the key to gently shifting anything we'd like to change in our relationship with our children.

REWIRING NOT IMPROVING

The good news is that no matter what our own current brain wiring is like, it is possible to change it. Doing so is a matter of practice and repetition. It's similar to physical exercise. If you use a muscle a few times it gets stronger. Then the exercise you're doing becomes easier for a while. You might decide to push it further. Each time you step it up or add to the resistance, there's a pain point where the next stage feels impossible. Yet the repetition eventually changes the impossible to possible, one small step at a time.

The brain behaves similarly to a muscle. The repetition of any activity, any thought or any feeling, strengthens that pathway until it becomes a new default setting, or until it feels easier.

After every outburst at the kids, I used to promise myself: *I am never*

ever going to shout at my kids like that again. You know how well that goes. When they set me off, all the good intentions in the world couldn't stop my brain, like a train, disappearing down the same familiar tracks in the heat of the moment.

So, what's left if love and great intentions aren't enough? For me, the discovery that my brain is wired to repeat patterns, rather than learn new ones, was massive. As the lights came on, I realised it was simply going to be a case of teaching my brain some new skills, rather than forcing some kind of moral improvement on my (to my mind) seriously lacking self.

HOW WE LEARN

The process of change is a natural one: as neural pathways and connections strengthen through repetition, others weaken through lack of use. Our brain follows this natural process of change whether we do it fast and furiously, or slowly and with a few false starts. It's a process that has four stages.

STAGE	SKILL LEVEL	OLD PATHWAY	NEW PATHWAY
1	Unaware unskilled	Existing	Not existing
2	Aware unskilled	Dominant	Existing
3	Aware skilled	Existing	Dominant
4	Unaware skilled	Dormant	Existing

I've come to love science, as long as it's easy to digest, and I like diagrams and processes when they clarify something for me. But I also have to translate them into my own words to make them stick. So for me it feels a little bit like this:

Stage 1: I'm on autopilot and it's not working

Stage 2: I'm aware of my patterns and it's still not working

Stage 3: I have a developing skill that's beginning to work

Stage 4: I'm on autopilot (mostly) with my new skill and it's working (mostly)

I sometimes imagine moving to a new country and learning a new language. I know that process would be filled with hope, then frustration at not being able to communicate, followed by moments of feeling competent in the new language, before time and immersion would eventually make it the most normal thing in the world. Moving from speaking English to speaking French is less loaded than moving from yelling to empathy, or from stress to calm, but the brain does it just the same way. It strengthens neural pathways through repeated use until that new structure is the dominant one – and you've developed a whole new skill.

I also like to use metaphor to help me to imagine the process. A few years ago, we moved house, and it took me about six weeks before I stopped taking the turn back to where we used to live. We travel down new roads and old roads. The new ones get wider in our subconscious brain until they become automatic in our conscious life. Similarly, computers often give us auto-correct suggestions according to our patterns of usage, and these follow our changes if they get repeated enough times. If you play a sport, dance, or play an instrument, you'll know how muscle memory retains the repetition of your practice, until you're able to do it without thinking.

I mentioned before about adopting this material in whatever way works for you. If the suggestions above don't resonate with you, find your own words, image or metaphor for the process of change. This deep understanding and personal connection to the idea of change as a process is likely to be helpful when things get harder, and you need to keep going through the messy second and third stages.

THE THREE BRAIN STATES

Our brain interprets every moment of our lives according to our past, our perceived present, our imagined future and even our changeable sense of self, rather than the moment itself holding any innate meaning. This explains why there can be as many different reactions to a situation as there are people involved.

Most of our reactions happen too fast for us to be consciously aware of the process that's taking place underneath. Instead we just see or experience the results. We feel joy, anger, sadness, fear; we think kind thoughts or judgmental ones; we shut down and hide, yell and shout, stop and listen, make lists and plan, work harder and harder, laugh and play or relax and rest. All of these responses and more can potentially happen to the same situation or event.

There is a simple way to understand the complexity of what's going on here. If you dig down through all the different layers of your brain – through the thoughts and emotions of your conscious mind, all the way down to the bottom of your subconscious mind – your brain will be in one of three main brain states. I call them red, orange and green.

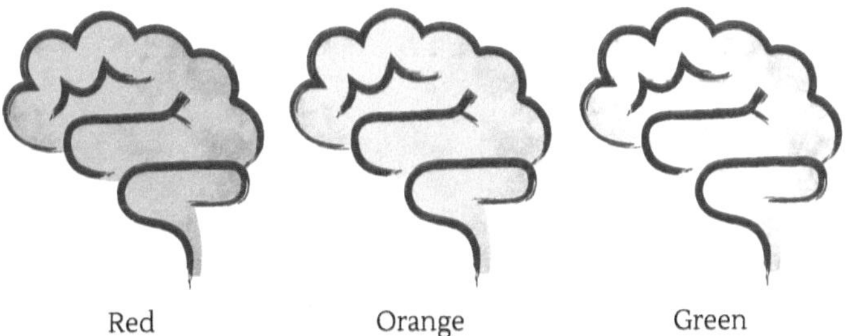

Red   Orange   Green

I'll explain further, but the first thing to understand is that these brain states exist on a spectrum or a continuum. You can be either extremely or mildly any one of these colours.

Whatever the intensity you're experiencing, all of your thoughts, feelings and actions – in each moment – will come from one of these brain states. So, let's take a look at what each of these states looks and feels like.

RED BRAIN

I want you to imagine for a moment that you've just seen a child run into the road and there's a car coming. (If this is too distressing for you, pick a different scenario that triggers feelings of intense stress). Imagining a scenario like this is uncomfortable, so we won't do this for long, but it may help to shut your eyes briefly to really feel the sensations. Notice firstly what's happening in your body. Next, think about or notice where your focus is and where it's not – are you aware of your surroundings or just the child and the oncoming car?

You'll probably be feeling some, or all, of the following physical and psychological shifts:

- Your heart rate goes up
- Your breathing speeds up
- Your muscles tense
- You may feel sweaty or tingly
- You get tunnel vision – you see the child and the car but nothing much else
- You feel fear and panic

Now imagine there's someone standing in your way as you race into the road to get the child. Notice what you do. It's likely you don't have a committee meeting with a passer-by to work out what should be done, nor do you politely ask the person in your way to move. Instead you make a quick judgment, push the person out of the way, and rescue the child as fast as you can.

Once you get back to safety, notice whether you feel calmer immediately, or whether you stay activated. Again, closing your eyes may help you pay attention to your body more easily. Physiologically your red-brain activation will start reducing, but it's likely to be hours before your body and emotions are back to normal.

Red brain is the 'fight-or-flight' brain-state, and it's been hard-wired into our brains through millions of years of evolution. It's the tiger-in-the-jungle brain and the hormones produced in our bodies while we're in red brain are cortisol and adrenaline. Red brain is the perfect brain state for emergencies. If it were my child in the road, I'd want your heart rate to go up and your muscles to be tense and ready for action. I'd want you to make a quick judgment and push past anyone in your way. This red-brain state is a useful automatic response. It's how our bodies are designed to keep ourselves, and others, safe. Every time there's real danger, our brain moves to fight-or-flight and then, when the danger is over, red brain reduces and our body and mind reset. It's a perfect design.

RED BRAIN
Name: Fight-or-flight
Hormones: Cortisol & adrenaline
Designed for: Emergencies

You may already see where this is going. Red brain exists on a spectrum and is triggered by anything you find stressful or threatening. It could be your email inbox, your bank statement, your two-year olds' tantrum, your teenager's door-slam or your own self-critical thinking. The intensity of red may be a little less, but our brain is producing the same hormones and triggering the same physiological and psychological responses. Unlike in a true emergency, we are now in exactly the wrong state for managing the situation.

When we are facing a non-emergency threat, we need a normal heart rate, normal breathing and relaxed muscles to be able to see the bigger picture. We need to access a kinder, more relational brain. Unfortunately, many parenting situations are tackled by two red brains – one older and one younger – both trying to get something they want to happen. Put yourself back in the physiological state of a red brain – the tense muscles, the sharp breaths, the tunnel vision – and you'll see how difficult it is to achieve a good outcome between two people in red brain. We're set up for either win or lose, fight or flight. Even if we, as the parent, 'win', it doesn't feel that good – and when our child 'wins', it feels even worse.

There are other things happening in our body during red brain that become problematic if this state is sustained, even at low levels, for long periods of time or if we visit it too regularly.

Things like:

- Increased blood pressure
- Suppressed immune system
- Reduced awareness of basic body functions like natural hunger and tiredness
- Weight gain
- Heart problems
- Headaches
- Digestive problems
- Disrupted sleep cycles
- Reduced sex drive
- Anxiety
- Depression
- Low self-esteem or loss of confidence
- Poor decision-making
- Difficulty in relationships

When I first learnt about red brain, so many lights went on for me. I realised I had been living in low-level red brain for a long time – probably from well before I had children – drip-feeding cortisol into my system. Despite having grown up in a very well-meaning home, my sister and I were expected to do as we were told, with little room to manoeuvre, and as a result, I had learnt unhelpful patterns of thinking from quite young. I was afraid of getting things wrong, which meant of course that I made mistakes much more often than a relaxed child does.

As I grew older, I developed a harsh internal critic, so I had my own red-brain hormones on tap. I lived with a fear of being told off or found out, which caused low-level anxiety day-in and day-out. I kept on top of it most of the time by being good at what I did, but it wasn't a peaceful existence.

For some, parenting is really their first experience of being triggered into red brain on a regular basis but, for me, children just intensified my experience of living close to the edge. I often jumped if one of my children screamed loudly, I got intensely cross if they spilt something that created extra work for me and, when they blazed through the house leaving a trail of stuff everywhere, I felt disrespected and taken for granted. It meant that in every moment of peace and fun with my family, stress and reactivity were just one small step away.

GREEN BRAIN

I want you to imagine for a moment that you're sitting somewhere peaceful and calm. Maybe it's your favourite spot in your home and you have a fresh coffee or cup of tea in hand, with time to do nothing, and your child or children are playing happily without needing your attention. This may feel like a stretch but give it a try. It may help to once again shut your eyes briefly and notice the sensations in your body, where your focus of attention is and any emotions you may be feeling. Come back to me when you're ready.

Welcome back. How was that?

You'll probably notice some, or all, of the following physical and psychological shifts:

- Your heart rate is normal (although after the red-brain exercise it may feel slow)
- Your breathing is normal or deeper
- Your muscles are relaxed
- Your awareness of both sight and sound has broadened out
- You may feel focused but not with tunnel vision
- You may feel calm, peaceful or content
- You may feel love or connection to your children
- You may feel gratitude or appreciation

Green brain exists at the opposite end of the spectrum to red. I call it the calm and present brain, or the cushioned brain, which is my way of describing the protection we feel in green brain from the inevitable triggers of our everyday lives. The hormones produced in our body in this state are serotonin, oxytocin and dopamine, all of which play different roles.

A simple understanding of each of the green-brain hormones has helped me appreciate what's going on when I experience green. I love each of these hormones and almost feel the subtle differences between them now as they come and go in my body.

- Serotonin is the feel-good, all-is-well hormone. It's the hormone at the heart of most anti-depressant medication and is connected to a sense of wellbeing and safety. At mild levels, serotonin simply feels 'normal' or maybe just a little more peaceful. In intensive bursts, it feels like deep joy and excitement.
- Oxytocin is the hormone related to relational connection. It's often over-branded as the romance hormone, but is actually activated whenever we make, or feel, a positive connection with another per-

son, or even a pet. When you think about your children when they're behaving well, or when they're asleep, you'll often feel oxytocin coursing through your system.

- Dopamine is the reward hormone. It's released when we feel motivated to do something, or when we feel like we've achieved something; it also helps reinforce healthy behaviours and is part of the process of strengthening neural pathways. After successfully rescuing the child in the road in our red-brain exercise, you will have had a download of dopamine.

In the exercise above, you might feel some or all of the following: serotonin because you're sitting and relaxing, oxytocin if your children's good behaviour makes you feel you really love them, and dopamine if you sense you must have done something right because now they're playing well without your intervention. If you felt all three, you're having a high-end green-brain moment.

The surprising thing about green brain is not so much its hormonal content, but what it is designed for. Despite how it feels, green brain is not the resting, relaxing or recovering brain; it's actually the normal, everyday brain. I gave you a high-end green-brain example – sitting in a relaxed environment with no demands on your time – because it's a good way to experience and understand what I mean by the green state.

GREEN BRAIN

Name:			Calm and present
Hormones:		Serotonin, oxytocin & dopamine
Designed for:		Everyday

Our bodies and our minds are perfectly designed to be calm and present and to live with green as our main brain state. When we consider some of the other things happening in our bodies while we are in green, it's clear that we function best physiologically, psychologically, and in our relationships with others when we're in a green-brain state. These things include:

- Normal blood pressure
- Normal heart rate
- Optimum immune system
- Increased awareness of basic body functions, such as hunger and tiredness
- Optimum digestive system
- Restored sleep cycles
- Healthy sex drive
- Healthy self-esteem
- Resilience
- Energy
- Self-confidence
- Good decision-making
- Creative problem-solving
- Better communication and negotiation skills
- Calm replaces stress as our deepest feeling
- Curiosity replaces control

The trick to understanding green brain is acknowledging that some situations are automatically and easily green: a happy child, the right football result, shared toys, a pay-rise, having time to sit and relax. Other situations are tricky, but not life-threatening: a delayed flight, a resistant child, a difference of opinion, a burnt dinner, an extensive to-do list. These day-to-day situations still require the psychological state, capabilities and physical responsiveness of green, but our brains tend to trigger the unsafe red state almost before we have time to stop it. We have to actively retrain our brain to return to green, so that we can better manage whatever we're dealing with.

We don't yet fully understand why our brains don't work that out for us and automatically distinguish between the situations that need tense muscles, tunnel vision and knee-jerk reactions, and the ones that are better handled with calm curiosity and creative problem-solving. What we do know is that there's a little organ in our brain called the amygdala, and its main job is to sense danger and respond accordingly by triggering cortisol and adrenaline into our system.

In many day-to-day situations our amygdala behaves like a badly positioned smoke alarm, located directly over the toaster, instead of in the hallway or corridor where it belongs. In this way, it keeps going off when there's no actual danger. Or, put another way, as parents we come under so much pressure that many of us feel as if our amygdala is on high alert a lot of the time. Because of this, we go into fight-or-flight mode quickly when our children are challenging.

For me, the discovery that I could train my brain to respond in a green-brain state to situations that would have typically triggered red was a revelation. We'll look at the practical ways to do this throughout this book, however I found that the initial understanding of the brain helped me through the process of change. I now realise that, with a little practice, I can be in green getting five children out the door in the morning, but I can also be in red brain while lying on the beach on holiday, if I let my thoughts run riot.

When we invest in the tools and green-brain practices that follow, our bodies, thoughts and emotions respond differently, and we are more in control of our brain state. With practice, we get to a point where, even in triggering moments, we don't have to work so hard to feel calm.

So, what does it look and feel like to be green in typically red situations?

My kids' difficult behaviours used to feel to me as if they were absolutely not OK. I used to dream of tidy, compliant little people in my house and, even more unhelpfully, assumed if I was a good enough parent, I would know how to achieve that. As my brain state has begun to change, I feel my own childhood not far away, and I see that when I behaved like that I was often responding out of both fear and frustration. Nowadays, conflict may not be entirely normal or neutral still, but it's closer to it and I know that it has no bearing on how good a parent I am.

Recently I was getting ready for work and it was spitting with rain. One of my nine-year-olds came in to ask if I would take them in the car, instead of making them walk as they usually do. I said I wouldn't, as it wasn't too wet. She asked again, and I felt her disappointment and frustration rising before she finally yelled, "You NEVER take us!"

In the past I would have risen to the bait and responded accordingly, because, of course, I take them often – when it's pouring, if they've got lots to carry, and every day I took them when they were little and so on. Or I would have explained why I had too much to do to take them. However, I was in green brain and felt real empathy for her, whilst still knowing I wasn't going to take her. I said something like, "It's really not fun having to walk when the weather's not so nice", which I really meant, as who wants to walk to school on a damp drizzly day? My daughter understandably stormed out of the room, as she hadn't had the answer she wanted. A few minutes later I heard, "Bye Mum, love you!" as she left for school.

This is just one example of how green is an internal state and not reliant on external circumstances. It feels as if there are fewer and fewer things that trigger reactivity in me, even when big emotions are involved. It's like having a cushion around me, which may not always be thick enough to provide protection from red brain, but often it is.

ORANGE BRAIN

Imagine you're sitting at home in the green-brain example mentioned earlier, but instead of feeling relaxed, you're alert waiting for the moment your kids start to fight, or you're problem-solving something or planning the day ahead in your mind. That's orange brain. It's not as intense as red – you're not managing threats and survival – but you're also not able to be fully present in the moment.

Just like the traffic lights, orange is in between red and green and is what I would refer to as the busy or goal-focused brain. It's the go-go-go brain and chances are high that you'll recognise it. On my Mindful Parenting course, I get to survey hundreds of parents and the majority identify with orange as their dominant brain state.

Orange brain makes a lot of lists, either literal ones or internal checklists. It's just a little bit ahead of itself all the time. It could be a few minutes ahead, like when you are thinking about your baby's next nap; a few days ahead, maybe focusing on Friday night; or, if you're a big planner or running your own business, it could even be a few years ahead. Orange brain also has what is referred to as 'monkey mind'; it jumps around all over the place and finds it hard to settle. In orange brain we tend to be slightly tense and a bit frowny. We move quickly and often get quite easily distracted. I'm convinced that when I'm in orange brain my list sometimes starts even before I wake up.

The question of why we seem to have become addicted to orange is not completely clear. Large-scale surveys across Europe and North America show that we feel busier, in general, than we used to. According to these surveys, we're more stressed at work and have less time to spend socially with family and friends. Interestingly though, further research actually shows our working hours haven't risen in the last few decades, and parents are spending more time with their children rather than less.[1] So, what's going on?

I find business psychologist Tony Crabbe's theory compelling. He says we now live in an "infinite world", [2] in which there's always more we can do – more emails to write and answer, more ideas to follow up on, more people to connect with and more meetings to go to. Not to mention the fact that you can knock one or two more things off your to-do list during a quick midnight online shop. Even when we're not working, the endless possibilities of what we could and should be doing with our downtime ultimately take away our feeling of relaxation.

We're finite beings, now living in a world of infinite possibilities, but those possibilities – instead of creating a sense of agency and freedom – are actually creating feelings of constant busyness, bordering on feelings of being overwhelmed. That's orange brain.

Apart from being a tricky brain state to live in, orange complicates our lives in three main ways.

ORANGE BRAIN

Name:	Busy/goal-focused
Problems:	Conditional
	Vulnerable to red
	Productivity myth

The first is that orange is a conditional brain state, which means it's planning to get to green (unlike red, which is too tunnel-focused to have green in its sights) but there are conditions to be met beforehand.

It's going to get there when...
... the renovations are finished
... the kids are asleep
... the kids are out of nappies
... the kids have all left home
... I've lost a few pounds
... I've got a new job
... the house is tidy
... I'm finally fit
You fill in your own blank.

The difficulty for many of us is that the list never stops. The weekly list gets swapped for the weekend list, or the endless-jobs-around-the-house list. Some of us are able to relax for a while on Friday night and find some time in green; others start thinking about the weekend as soon as Friday night hits. *What do good families do on Saturdays? They're all out biking together, we'd better get the punctures fixed.*

The next challenge is that orange brain makes us very vulnerable to red. Orange brain is goal-focused, so unless you're really in control of your goals, you're highly likely to get triggered. In parenting, we not only have more goals to achieve overall, but our children tend to have very little interest in helping us meet them. Keeping the house tidy, being on time, looking good in public and getting a good night's sleep, are not things most children are concerned about, so when we parent in orange, we get triggered into red on a regular basis.

I was recently driving a friend's pre-schooler home when the little girl pointed to the roadworks and the detour on her street and said excitedly that they made her mummy say the 'F-word'. I loved her for the frank confessions that little people so effortlessly make, and for reminding me how easily that could have been one of my children, describing me to their friends' parents. It's an orange-brain situation that most of us can recognise; we react suddenly and can't help ourselves because our goal – in this case of getting somewhere on time – has just been thwarted.

For me, getting out the door in the mornings on time with five children was a goal that almost always made me see red, unless all of them happened to do the right thing, at the right speed, on the same day, which was pretty rare. I hated the morning carnage, and whether I used sticker charts, rewards, threats or consequences, nothing worked for any length of time because I was starting in orange, so red brain was never far away.

When our goals are larger than getting the kids to bed, or out the door – for example, building a successful business, having a great family or in some way improving ourselves – our reactions in the moment may not seem to be affected. However, if we sense our goal isn't being achieved the way we'd like, we can have an underlying sense of failure or frustration that is hard to shift and prevents us from being fully present. This is a subtler version of what orange brain feels like.

Apart from being conditional and vulnerable to red brain, the final challenge with orange – and my personal favourite – is a phenomenon called the productivity myth. At its heart, the productivity myth suggests that orange is not as productive as green. As counterintuitive as that may sound, we actually get more done in green brain than we do in orange brain.

Research shows that we lead more productive lives in green than in orange because our brains are sharper, our bodies are healthier, and our relationships are richer. In green brain we are calmer and more creative. We take fewer sick days, negotiate well with difficult colleagues or children, and fail and try again. We stay curious and more flexible; we're less judgmental, we believe in ourselves more, we keep our boundaries clear, and we find it easier to know when to rest.

Increasingly, high-performance companies and international sports teams are introducing green-brain activities into their more naturally orange work environments. For example, mindfulness (which we'll look at in more detail in Chapter Two) is now an integral part of employee development at companies like Goldman Sachs, Google, Apple and Nike. This move is not primarily out of concern for wellbeing, but because green brain increases productivity and performance.

Parenting is no different. It's highly intense, tending towards orange brain, and is as much in need of green-brain training as any other high-performance environment.

A WORD ABOUT SUCCESS

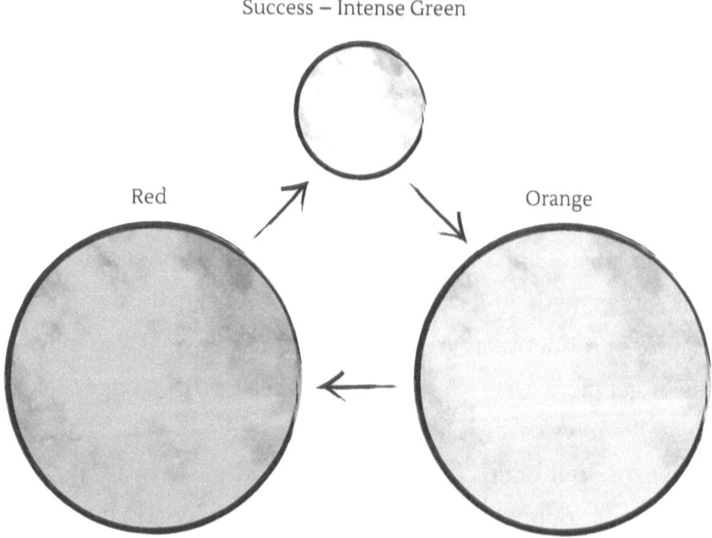

The Addictive Success Cycle

One of the reasons many of us sustain a cycle of living in orange as our main brain state – with occasional or frequent dips in and out of red is because of something I call the 'addictive success cycle'. Success is a highly addictive, temporary green-brain state that breaks the orange/red cycle briefly. When we achieve success, we get a release of dopamine – that reward hormone we talked about earlier – which gives us just enough motivation to keep going.

Maybe you've worked twelve hours a day at your start-up for a year and you're finally beginning to outstrip your competitors. Or perhaps you've nagged your child for months to focus on their homework or their scales, and they're now doing better at school or are a better piano player. Your hours at work may be affecting your family life, and your relationship with your child is suffering from all the nagging, but you get the success hit of high-intensity serotonin and dopamine, so it feels as if what you're doing is working. Seemingly justified, you keep going in orange – detouring in and out of red, with an occasional green-brain success high, and the cycle begins again.

If we could strip our brains back to their most simple chemistry, we would see that our brain struggles with too much cortisol and adrenaline when we spend long periods of time in orange or red brain. We've seen how cortisol and adrenaline affect everything from our muscles, to our digestion, to our sleep cycles – so the relief and joy that the dopamine and serotonin from success brings is highly addictive, simply because we aren't getting enough of those for our bodies to feel healthy. It's not necessarily because we're really ambitious or need our children to do better than others, it's simply because our brains desperately need the hormone shift. In other words, we are in real need of some green-brain hormones to balance out our system.

In green brain, success is more like a pattern than an addictive cycle. We tend to experience more success – partly because our brains work better, but also because our definition of success broadens out, so that we experience it in new ways and more consistently.

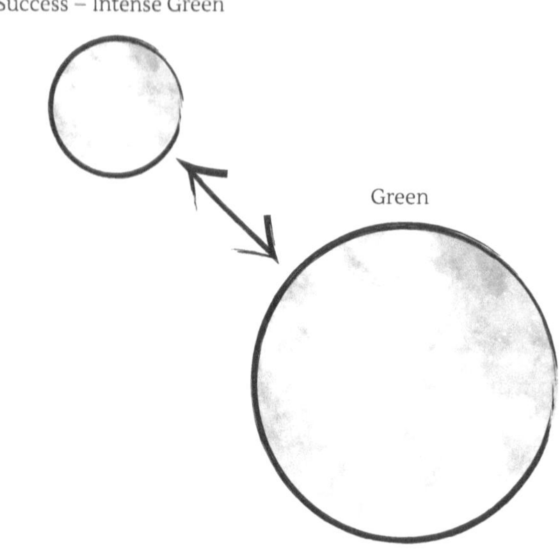

The Success Pattern

At a hormonal level, our experience of success may not be as intense because, on a normal day, our brain already has a healthy amount of dopamine and serotonin. However, this success spike is also less addictive, more sustainable over many years, and it doesn't come at the expense of our relationships.

There's a certain irony to exploring new ideas like this and then taking precious time to do exercises like the ones that follow. Even reading this book may be a stretch because you've got so many other things you could be doing. But knowing what state your brain is in, and then when and how it lights up with which colour, is at the heart of shifting to green as your primary state. Consider the following four questions to start getting some insight into the way your own brain operates, and, as you do so, curiosity will keep you in green brain and help you avoid taking a task-focused orange-brain approach to the exercise.

INSIGHT QUESTIONS · BRAIN STATES

What brain state is your home base – which one do you spend the most time in?

You can add intensity here. For example, mine was low-level red when I first answered this question.

What are your patterns? How and when do you move between the three states?

A helpful way to approach this is to think about which relationships trigger you into a certain colour, and which situations, or times of the day. For example, you may be green with one child and red with another. You may be green at work and orange or red at home (or vice versa). You may be red when the kids are going to bed and green by the time it's your bedtime.

How do these patterns affect your life?

Think about these specific areas: Parenting? Other key relationships? Health and well-being? Happiness?

Currently what gets you to green?

This is likely to be favourite relationships, favourite activities or favourite places.

The most common pattern I see is parents who live in an orange-brain state and tip into red from time to time, which is like driving a car with the handbrake on. The aim of all the activities in this book is to build your awareness and then empower you to build your green-brain cushion, so you can drive more smoothly and easily, no matter what life throws at you.

On one of my courses, a brave dad raised his hand after he wrote his answers down, and said he'd had a revelation about his relationship with his children, which at the time was proving to be a real struggle for him.

He had looked at the pattern of each day and realised that he woke up orange, and generally moved into red while he and his partner tried to get themselves and the kids ready and out of the door on time. It's a familiar pattern to many of us. He was mostly green at work because he liked his job, but he was tired by the end of the day and usually arrived home ready for a rest. He enjoyed the first few minutes of interaction with his children, but their demands for his time, and all the jobs that home life brings soon moved him into red. After the stress of getting his children to bed, he would then go green for a while as he relaxed in front of the TV.

His revelation was that, although his day felt manageable because he got plenty of green, the time he spent with his kids was almost exclusively orange or red.

As a result, he made some changes to his routine. The morning remained a struggle, as it does in many homes, but after work changed. He decided, with the agreement of his partner, that he would walk around the park after work to clear his head. That meant he would arrive home a few minutes later, but that he would be ready for time with his children rather than ready to collapse. Within a few days of doing this, he noticed changes. He started to get more cuddles and have more fun. He felt more energy and even started to look forward to coming home, and to the things he and his kids would do together.

As his children got more green-brain time with their dad, there were noticeable shifts in their behaviour too. He now describes them as being far less demanding, more likely to do what he asks and with less resistance, and more fun to be around. In the following chapters you'll see that green-brain time is not only more enjoyable for us, but it also relaxes our children's growing brains, which significantly impacts their responsiveness, resilience, confidence and so much more.

2. Mindfulness really matters

This is my simple religion.
There is no need for temples; no need for complicated philosophy.
Our own brain, our own heart is our temple:
the philosophy is kindness.

~ The Dalai Lama

Forever is composed of nows

~ Emily Dickinson

Living our lives in a permanent green-brain state is not the aim here; that's just not realistic. Life is busy, finances may be tight, it feels like there's never enough time and our children are surrounded by things they believe they need to be happy, as are we. Unless you plan to hop off the grid, it's likely that stress will be a regular part of your life. My passion is helping parents to get just a bit greener, or to shift just enough so that green becomes a default setting or home-base, so that our brains and our bodies are more regularly in the state they were designed for.

Although it's important at any stage of our lives, we have so many more reasons to find our green brain when we become parents. Before I had kids, I was really the only one affected by my own negative comparisons and self-criticism. I could handle that, mostly, although it wasn't much fun. Once I became a parent, the stakes got much higher. My red and orange brain started to have an impact on my children.

Despite our best intentions, we can't hide the colour of our brain, no matter how hard we try. Our kids really don't listen to much of what we say, if you hadn't noticed. They watch us and they sense us; they feel what it's like to be around us. Even if our brain is in orange because of all the opportunities we want for our children, or our well-meaning busyness is for a good cause, green is the relational brain and what our children need from us so they can thrive.

The bottom line is that we parent out of overflow, not out of intention. Our inner world has a greater impact on how we parent than any of the ideas we have about how we'd like to parent. No matter how much we want our children to have a great childhood and a green-brained childhood, the colour of our brain determines the colour of our home.

This isn't supposed to load you with any additional parental guilt. It's actually really good news, because our children can be the catalyst for a better life for us. We may have given up living from green for ourselves because a better salary, nicer house, or more time on social media are just too tempting – or because we've forgotten how to prioritise time for ourselves, or have grown up so used to self-critical thinking that it feels normal – but most of us would do almost anything for our children.

What I love is that the best thing for them happens to be the best thing for us too.

GETTING TO GREEN: EXTERNAL GREEN

The first way of cultivating more green-brain time is to prioritise the people or activities that already get us there. These are the things and the people that you wrote for the final question at the end of the last chapter. I call these sources of 'external green'. Exercise, a healthy diet, good friends and regular sleep are all high on the list of helpful green-brain strategies, but anything that you enjoy and that brings you a sense of well-being is worth adding to, or increasing in, your life as much as possible.

Often we think that an evening out, a yoga class, a trip away or buying food that's just for us is self-indulgent and that it takes time or money away from so-called more important things, like work or the kids. However, those things are not just for relaxation; they promote good, life-long physical and mental health, as well as enhanced relationships, because all of these are improved by spending time in green.

Your children need your green brain, more than they need your presence. If your child dislikes babysitters, but you relax and recharge when you go out for a child-free evening, then get a babysitter and go out. Of course, make sure the babysitter is someone you know and trust but, assuming they are, your child will benefit more than you realise, and the short-term upset will ultimately be worth it.

If you're parenting with a partner, a great way to sustain green in your home is to see if you can help each other do whatever feels like fun for each of you outside of the home. This doesn't necessarily mean an all-hours pass to the golf course but asking what works for each of you is as important to your kids' healthy development as the family time you have together. If you're parenting on your own, this aspect can be harder, but I know of two solo parents who take turns to have each other's children once a week, so each of them can commit to something regularly that helps them get a green-brain break.

If you've forgotten what you used to enjoy before you had kids, it's time to remind yourself – or find something a little more practical if arctic exploration or skydiving was your thing.

With five kids, our time and budget has been quite limited, so the things I do are very simple. Every fortnight on a Monday evening I hang out with one of my best friends, and my partner hangs out with her partner. No babysitters are involved, although Shiraz and chocolate often are. We swap houses, and that's the only change. It feeds my brain with green and I look forward to it every time.

I also love good drama (when it's on screen), and now that going to the cinema is mostly not an option, I watch good drama at home. I don't just flick the TV on though. I do my research and choose something that only I will love (usually a little dark and depressing, which just happens to be my style). The anticipation produces as much green as the actual experience.

Finally, I also love running. I always have, even as a little girl. I've been told my version is called 'jogging', but I'm sticking with running. It's been a real challenge to find a way to fit it in, but I now run in the mornings, which is well planned because, by the time I'm home, my partner has done the tricky job of getting the kids up. He then swims after work, so it's my turn at the other end of the day to hold the fort.

None of these things cost much, and all of them happen regularly enough that I always have something to look forward to that isn't too far away. You may already be doing lots of things you love, in which case you can just add to that the joy of knowing it's really good for your children when you do.

All of these are great; however, the reality is that – while parenting – external activities are not enough to protect us from being triggered with our children. When it's all going badly, we can't just leave them to it and go out for a drink or settle down to a good TV drama (although it's tempting). That's why there has to be another way.

GETTING TO GREEN: INTERNAL GREEN

The other way we get to green is through brain training. I call this 'internal green' and it offers us the sort of sustainability that external green simply can't. For me, having access to internal green is like having a superpower. It's when we dig deep and discover that we can, with a little practice, get to green anytime, because it's our natural brain state. I often think of this state as patiently waiting just beneath my flitting and darting orange brain, or my edgy or apprehensive red one. In this way, the movement towards green is closer to archaeology than architecture. It's about turning our attention to what's already there underneath, as opposed to trying to construct something new to add to our lives.

One of the very best ways to develop the life-long skill of green-brain living is through mindfulness. It's free, it's always available, and the research behind its effectiveness is now overwhelming. Well over 3,000 studies are showing promising results in terms of the effectiveness of mindfulness. [1] Although more studies need to be done for us to know more about how and why our brains respond as they do, so far there are strong indications that all of the following improve with regular mindfulness practice:

- Learning
- Memory
- Productivity
- Creativity
- Enjoyment

- Emotion regulation
- Immunity
- Sleep
- Sex
- Concentration
- Empathy
- Compassion
- Self-confidence
- Relationships
- Social skills.

On the other side of this, mindfulness has been found to reduce:

- Stress
- Reactivity
- Depression
- Anxiety
- Anger
- Loneliness
- Blood pressure
- Inflammation
- Impulsivity
- PTSD
- OCD
- Substance abuse
- Eating disorders

So how does one thing have such a far-reaching impact? And if all of the evidence is there, how come so many of us have no idea we have a green-brain solution at our fingertips?

MY OWN JOURNEY WITH MINDFULNESS

I came across mindfulness as part of my counselling training a few years ago. It was one of the ways I was encouraged to work with clients and become better at my job. At the time, I had no understanding of brain states or neuroplasticity, and I couldn't put the pieces together in my mind. I like things to be practical or have a direct application, and I couldn't understand how paying attention to my breathing, or chewing a raisin slowly would help me, or my clients, in our everyday lives. Suffice to say, I didn't pursue mindfulness.

When mindfulness is explained without referring to the chemical shifts that take place in our brains, it often makes sense only to those who are already drawn to 'being in the moment'. For them, it's an easy sell. For the rest of us, we need something more. If we're trying to be less stressed but still get all the things done that we need to, surely it makes sense to become more efficient or more competent rather than slow down and pay attention to the small things? It took me a second introduction to discover that, with mindfulness, we can slow down, become calmer, grow in happiness, deepen our relationships and still get more done, which is a win-win in my book.

The reason mindfulness is a unique way to de-stress and improve our wellbeing is that it's not a thing we do – like yoga, exercise, a new diet or even a parenting strategy – it's a way of being in the world. It's how we do what we are doing. We can exercise mindfully, we can eat mindfully, we can listen to our children mindfully, and equally, we can do all of these things mindlessly. Mindfulness is more than an activity; it triggers deeper shifts in our brain. If you remember back to the idea of neuroplasticity, you'll understand that over time it also retrains our brain, which transforms how we do, or don't do, everything we do.

SO, WHAT REALLY IS MINDFULNESS?

Mindfulness is made up of two main components: attention and attitude. We'll look at each of these in turn.

ATTENTION - TAMING THE MONKEY MIND

As I've mentioned, monkey mind is the term we use to describe the way our minds jump from thought to thought and idea to idea, without us really choosing what we're focusing on. To many of us this feels completely normal, and we live as if that's just the way adult life works. It's also one of the most common characteristics of orange brain.

Living with monkey mind has a subtle but destructive impact on our happiness. One of the most significant impacts of monkey mind is that our brain uses up energy every time we shift attention. The tiredness we feel at the end of a day of juggling numerous things in our brain is very real. Even though we sometimes call it multitasking, our brains can't actually focus properly on more than one thing at a time. It should probably more accurately be called 'very-fast-and-inefficient-brain-jumping', which is a bit of a mouthful and probably why multitasking is preferred.

Not only do we use up much-needed energy when our brain jumps around, we also now know that this rapid movement in our brains releases the stress hormones cortisol and adrenaline, so monkey mind is associated with red brain as well as orange.

In monkey mind, we're rarely enjoying great memories and looking forward to the future as our brain skips around. What we're more often doing is scanning the past for regret and the future for threat. It's like having a radar in our brain, with the signal scanning for enemy aircraft. It often starts just before we wake up: blip blip blip. We then whizz around clearing all the threats (drop offs, pickups, deadlines, our email inbox, life admin, unhappy kids) hoping the scan will clear. If we're lucky it does for an hour or so as we relax in the evening, before starting it all over again the next day. If we're not so lucky, we carry some of these blips to bed with us, and then add them to new ones the following day.

Mindfulness offers a radically different approach. Instead of constantly looking for, and working to clear, all the threats, we learn how to keep the radar beam still. We learn to pay attention in the present moment to the present moment. This sounds so simple, but it's so difficult to do.

A large-scale study conducted in the US discovered a direct link between paying attention to the present moment and feelings of happiness.[2] Predictably, participants rated their happiness higher when they were paying attention to a pleasant present than when they were letting their minds wander to something that was worrying them. The big surprise, however, was that those paying attention to an unpleasant present – in this case their morning commute – experienced slightly higher levels of happiness than when they were thinking about something else that was good or positive. The research concluded that having the ability to pay attention to the present moment, whether that moment is pleasant or unpleasant, was key to the experience of happiness.

Despite it being so important to our wellbeing, most of us spend very little time with our brain and our body in the same place at the same time. Even brief moments of stillness in our mind produce bite-size pieces of calm and contentment.

Mindfulness doesn't mean we never look back or plan ahead. When we're able to still our minds in the present, our reflections about the past have a purpose to them – like growth, awareness or letting go of something – and our planning for the future is a real activity, not an ocean of worries.

Before we move on to the second component of mindfulness, I want to share one final thought about monkey mind. Kids aren't natural monkey-minders, especially when they're little. They live in the moment. They focus on one thing at a time, spend a lot of time in green brain and move rapidly to red when they're upset, and back again quickly. Despite experiencing regular red brain, they generally have less stress in their brains overall because they're mostly monotasking. Monkey mind and orange brain are more adult territory, with some teenagers more vulnerable to a busy multitasking brain than others.

Ironically, our children's natural ability to be in the moment is often why we, as parents, experience more stress. We desperately try to get them to multitask to make our lives easier. I would love to remind my children of ten things they need to do before we leave the house and have them remember all of them, or have them notice their pile of clothes on the stairs instead of tripping over them and muttering about the obstruction in the middle of their race track.

Later in the book we'll explore how we manage the practicalities of life without overwhelming our children's playful, relational brain. For now, it's a helpful start simply to understand that monkey mind – the busy brain – is not a great state for any of us to be in, and especially not our children.

We've looked at what we're paying attention to. The second component of mindfulness is how we pay attention.

ATTITUDE · TAMING THE INNER CRITIC

The biggest triggers in our daily lives come from our internal world, not our external world. What we're triggered by is actually not that such-and-such did this, or so-and-so didn't do that; our reactions, and the changes in our brain state come from the constant stream of shoulds and shouldn'ts, and of comparisons, that are set in motion often by external events. This is the internal dialogue that's attached to monkey mind.

When we compare ourselves with others, we mostly find ourselves lower down whichever comparison ladder we've chosen. This stimulates the production of cortisol and stress in our system. Even when we find ourselves higher up the ladder, it's no more helpful to our brain. Our perceived success may produce a brief blast of the happy hormones, but comparisons don't truly develop green brain in any sustainable way.

Some of us have our inner critic directed towards others, which is effectively red brain in fight mode. Some of us keep our shoulds and shouldn'ts mostly for ourselves, which is red brain in flight mode. Criticism of others isn't a sign of confidence; it's simply a reflection of what's going on inside. If you wake up feeling really good about yourself, you'll have plenty of cushioning around yourself and those you live with. You'll generally be able to find ways to work with even the most resistant toddler or teenager. If you stumble out of bed sensing the weight of a deadline, or the extra pounds you've put on, you will barely make it through your bedroom door before you find someone in your home deeply irritating.

Of course, it's easier to be around a flight person than a fight person, but it's not a sign of humility, maturity or green brain when we find fault with ourselves while praising others. It's the inner critic hard at work in the same way – just a little more hidden.

When we live consistently in orange brain, often the only time we keep our monkey mind still is when we're ruminating on something negative. We chew it over and over. Our mind is attentive and focused – which is mindfulness component number one – but it's also negative and critical. The second component is missing. The attitude with which we pay attention is just as important as the focus itself.
The three attitudes at the heart of mindfulness are:

- Kindness
- Curiosity
- Non-judgmentalism

As soon as you activate any of these three attitudes, your brain senses something is right. It senses safety. It lowers the defences. As a result, healthy hormones are released, and our stress hormones are reduced. As you might imagine, the opposite is also true: as soon as we feel a judgmental thought, our brain senses something isn't right and releases cortisol. Our judgments can be constant and might go almost entirely undetected.

Some of mine sound like this:

> *My kids have no idea how lucky they are.*
> *I don't have enough time.*
> *Why doesn't anyone listen to me?*
> *I shouldn't have had that extra coffee.*
> *Why don't my kids play nicely together?*
> *Why do I do all the work?*
> *They have had far too much screen time.*
> *How come that child is so good at... or is so polite... ?*
> *I've no idea what to cook for dinner.*

These thoughts may seem innocent enough. They may even seem helpful. None of them are. Each of these thoughts shoots cortisol into my system, which either turns into action fuelled by annoyance, or inaction fuelled by resentment or frustration.

When we start to practice attitudes of kindness and curiosity, mindfulness begins to tame the inner critic, just as it tames the monkey mind. The shoulds and shouldn'ts, and the negative commentary, are slowly replaced by an awareness and acceptance of the present without judgment.

It may be hard to read this without wondering what on earth might happen in your family if you don't identify areas that need to be improved? What if you end up settling for a life that's not as good as it could be, or become the maid doing all the work? It's a valid concern, and makes so much sense. However, the exact opposite is true. Let's take a look at why.

When we judge or criticise anything, our thought processes come from a red-brain state, so any improvements we make are fuelled by the need to manage some kind of threat. We may grow in a skill, our children may come off their screens and get down to their homework, but it doesn't make our lives or theirs more healthy or enjoyable because becoming more successful doesn't necessarily offer us green. When we refuse to judge and instead get curious and kind, our thoughts are coming from a place of safety. Our brain then works entirely differently.

In green brain, the journey is far more important than the outcome, and any scorecards or comparisons take a back seat. I'm a counsellor, I'm a mum and I'm a person; I have no idea (nor much interest) in how I rank in my professional world, the world of parenting, or any other world. On a really green-brain day I have a sense of freedom, of energy and of productivity that's the total opposite of feeling unmotivated or of settling, or of comparing with others. There's a flow that seems to occur naturally.

Because our brains are wired for growth and development, we will never stay static when our brains are in a healthy state. For our children, the judgments we make towards them and the drive to improve them or change them often causes the very opposite to happen. No matter how nervous we are about our kids' approaches to life or their struggles, when we quieten our inner critic and instead offer curiosity and kindness, they are much more likely to find their wings and excel at whatever they're wired for.

Just to whet your appetite for reading on, I have been stunned to watch my children not just discover how lucky they are, but also come to share the load of the jobs at home, find resilience around things they don't want to do, and manage their lives really well. Of course they're not like this all the time − that would be a little weird. They're ordinary kids with strong emotions, healthy resistance and selective hearing. But since I stepped back from trying to make it all happen and stopped living in full orange (tipping into red) brain, there's been a significant change in them. Green has remarkable knock-on effects.

You will, no doubt, find lots of complicated definitions of mindfulness. Mine is remarkably simple:

Mindfulness is (PACK)

Paying
Attention with
Curiosity and
Kindness

If you pay attention (taming the monkey mind) with curiosity and kindness (taming the inner critic) you are already being mindful. Your brain is learning to function in the way it was designed to.

Just for a minute now, focus on something around you with curiosity and without any judgment. It could be your home, this book, a tree, the rain, your coffee, your child's face, even your pile of washing that you may have been avoiding looking at. Take a few seconds and really notice. Take in the texture of paper, the warmth of the sun on your skin, the smells of the room. Your nerve endings are lighting up with every sensation. You are alive, and present.

It may be fleeting, but you'll find green-brain hormones are instantly released with a mindfulness exercise like this. Even the pile of dirty clothes will bring a small measure of green brain. Yes, they may still need to be washed, but the people you love wear these clothes (the realisation of which triggers oxytocin) and you have enough money to buy them (which stimulates serotonin and dopamine). Even that's not so bad.

For mindfulness to become a way of life, we need to practice it. Trying to engage mindfulness at random moments, and especially in stressful situations, is really difficult to do. To develop the skill, we have to redesign the pathways of our brain, which we do by engaging in small amounts of regular practice, on a daily basis.

It really is so similar to exercise. When we go to the gym, for example, we don't walk around and check out the equipment and then go home, feeling much better, because we've understood what each piece of kit does for our body. We hop on and get going. We also know that the more often we go the fitter we become. We can go as often or as seldom as we like, but repetition is the key to sustainable development. Brain training is really no different.

For me, developing a mindfulness practice – and, ultimately, a more mindful way of living – has been slow but incremental, and it's a journey I will continue to do all my life. I still get stressed and find life and parenting challenging, but green is now my home base and finding my way back there gets easier and easier. I also recognise more quickly when I've been stuck in orange for a few hours or I've got lost deep in red-brain anxiety and stress.

I've had a perfect example of this now as I work on this book.

I just sat back in the middle of writing because I could feel the cortisol creeping up. I'm in a café and it's my writing morning, but it's just not happening today. I've been typing faster than usual and deleting more than I've written. My shoulders are tense. I'm aware that I'm also procrastinating because I need to go and do the food shopping before the kids get home. I probably look green on the outside. I look like one of those creatives who sits around drinking coffee and musing on life. However, I'm no greener than the mum at the next table who is begging her kids to stop whining and colour in their pictures.

As I stop for a moment to sit back and notice, I see the trees outside and feel the breeze through the window. I take a deep breath, scan the faces of the people around me and a glimmer of green breaks through the orangey-red. I've written what I've written. There are no shoulds that will help me now. I didn't get the enjoyable dopamine fix I got last week from my writing (external green), but I can either fill up with cortisol by criticising myself, or with serotonin by accepting today just as it's happening (internal green).

Maybe it sounds overly romantic, but I have a tendency towards perfectionism. Whatever I'm doing, I'll find a way to do it in low-level red if I'm left to my own devices. I've had to consciously learn to do things differently. I have a regular practice, which I will end this chapter by guiding you through. I also have to stop, regularly and intentionally during my day, and be mindful of the moment, in order to get back to my green home base.

Before I introduce you to a simple mindfulness practice, I first want to mention just some of the changes that take place in our brain when mindfulness becomes a regular activity.

In a recent study, MRI scans were taken of participants before and after an eight-week course of regular mindfulness practice. These physical changes were seen, and measured, in the brains of the participants.

- The amygdala, which is the seat of the stress response, reduced in size.
- The hippocampus, which is the seat of learning and memory, increased in size. This is especially significant because the hippocampus is also the part of the brain that shrinks when we experience depression.

- The temporo-parietal area, which is the seat of creativity, compassion and empathy, also increased. [3]

I would love to have taken an MRI of my brain before I embarked on my journey with mindfulness, and be able to compare that to one now, just a few years later. I'm convinced that many of those changes have taken place in my own brain.

The scientific evidence behind the benefits of mindfulness has helped me time and time again to return to a regular practice. The brain naturally works both for us and against us in the development of any new habit. Although my brain thrives on mindfulness, and positive structural change takes place in my brain as I do it, my brain also loves repetition, which means it will resist any new practice – no matter how healthy – until it becomes familiar. So we need all the help we can get to persuade ourselves to practice. I often imagine the subtle evolution taking place in my brain when I pay attention to my breathing or the sounds and sights around me.

INTRODUCING SIX CORE MINDFULNESS SKILLS

Throughout this book I'm going to introduce you to six core skills. Three of these will train you, as parents, to enjoy your own life more. The other three are relational skills for you to use with your children. First, in line with the fact that we start with ourselves, is a mindfulness practice based around our breath and senses.

The reason we start with breath and senses when we practice mindfulness is that we always have access to them. Wherever we are, this is the simplest way to bring your attention to the present moment. You can do the following exercise sitting down, or on the go, whether you're walking, running, driving, eating, even in the shower. You can just focus on your breath for the whole exercise, you can choose just one sense, or do the full exercise. There are no rules, other than paying attention with curiosity to whatever you've chosen. And you just keep returning to that attention when your mind wanders – which it will, over and over again.

CORE SKILL 1:
MINDFULNESS OF THE BREATH & SENSES

BREATH:

Take a deep breath, and, as you breathe out, drop your shoulders and relax. You may find it helpful to close your eyes as long as it's safe to do so.

Take another deep breath and, as you breathe out, drop your shoulders and relax.

Take one more deep breath. Relax your eyebrows, relax your cheek muscles, relax your jaw. As you breathe out, drop your shoulders again and see if you can fully relax.

Notice your chest rising and falling as you breathe in and breathe out. Notice what happens in your body as you breathe in and out. Keep breathing in and out slowly, paying attention to each breath.

Each time your thoughts wander off, gently and kindly bring them back to your breath.

See if you can pay attention to your breath from the beginning of the inhale to the end of the exhale.

You may be able to feel green brain kicking in as you pay attention with curiosity and kindness to your breath.

You may feel gratitude for your breath and the fact you are alive.

You may feel nothing.

Keep bringing your thoughts gently and kindly back to your breath.
You can stay focused just on your breathing or turn your attention to
your senses.

SENSES:

Turn your attention to what you can see. (Only use sight as a mindful
sense if you are somewhere that doesn't stimulate your orange brain.
Outside in nature is often great for this).

Focus on one thing at a time and pay attention with curiosity. See if you
notice things you don't usually pay attention to. Just observe and describe to yourself what you see.

Now turn your attention to what you can hear. If it's safe to do so, shut
your eyes. Notice sounds in the distance and nearby. See if you notice
any sounds you haven't noticed before.

Next move your focus to how you physically feel. Without judgment, notice your body on the chair or the movement of your limbs as you walk.
Feel the fresh air on your skin, or the texture of your clothing. Notice any
stress or pain, without trying to change or fix anything at all.

Now pay attention to what you can taste or smell. These senses are most effective when you're eating or drinking. Really smell your coffee and taste your food. Smell is also effective when you're in nature. Linger where you are and notice the scents of the sea, the trees, or the flowers.

As you pay attention to each sense, bring your attention back – gently and kindly – each time your thoughts wander off somewhere else.

Return to your breath at the end of the exercise, finishing with three deep breaths. See if you can pay attention to one, two or even all three breaths from the beginning of the inhale to the end of the exhale.

When you're ready, slowly open your eyes and return your attention to your day.

COMMITTING TO YOUR PRACTICE

As you can see, you can practice this exercise anywhere, anytime. That said, because our brains love repetition, choosing the same place and time will make it much easier to develop a regular practice. Read the exercise through completely and just choose parts of it initially. You'll find it becomes second nature pretty quickly, and you won't need to read it each time.

Some people find their thoughts settle quickly, while others find it much harder to calm their monkey mind. Neither is right nor wrong, nor better. We need both skills – the ability to keep our mind still, and the ability to continually bring our focus back to where we want it to be.

I hear so many parents say they're not good at mindfulness. They find the attention piece hard, so then the attitude of kindness collapses too. One of the best things I was ever taught is that each time we return our thoughts back to our breath or to one of our senses, we're widening the green-brain pathway in our brain and doing something great for our health. If your thoughts wander 100 times in a few minutes, and you bring them back each time, then you've done 100 good things for your brain in just a few minutes. When was the last time you did that many helpful things in such a short space of time?

My other recommendation would be to not make your practice too hard initially. Start with five minutes or, if that's too long, start with three. It's better to want to do more than less. If you enjoy it, you may decide to extend it.

I took a while to work out what worked best for me. It still makes me laugh when I think about that awkward period of experimenting with my 'happy place'. I moved around from the bean bag to the sofa, trying to find my spot and thinking about what people look like on Instagram when they meditate; you know there's a certain light that seems to come in and dance across the space! Hopefully you won't be as fussy as I was.

There's no need to sit either. You can be on the move or be anywhere. You just have to be intentional, and choose your time and place consciously, for it to become a regular practice.

I discovered the beanbag works for me. Every morning, after the kids have left for school, I make myself a coffee and sit on my beanbag before I see my first client of the day. I follow the practice above, adapting it for the day and for how I feel. Sometimes I keep simply to my breath, other times I add in one or more of my senses too. I've extended my practice a little, and I see one less client a day because of it, but it takes me a while to settle. I love the peace I feel when I finally do though, and I find I'm more productive if I've started my day this way. I wouldn't be without my mindful practice now – it's an anchor point of my day.

I have a client who does her practice at the point when the traffic slows to a halt every day on her way to and from work. It's just a few minutes, twice a day, she sits and pays attention (I presume with her eyes wide open.) She's told me that she's loving the changes to her stress levels, so she's added a few minutes at lunchtime – when she stops to pay attention to the view from her window, creating pockets of internal green throughout her day. A dad I've been working with has chosen the creative approach of listening to a piece of music he loves at full volume. Fully immersing himself in what he can hear is a total luxury for him, and he comes out glowing with green.

Another client, who is with her children all day, practices for a few minutes in the evening once the kids are down and before she checks her Facebook feed. She alternates between walking around the block if her partner's home or sitting in a chair she's chosen if he's not, so there's not too much variation. She's found her interest in social media waning, as she's noticed her brain shifts from green to orange when she goes online. Some evenings she now settles without needing to check in with what the world around her has been up to.

It might feel like a slow process, because often nothing really happens during our practice. Typically, the benefits of mindfulness practice are experienced in the other moments of our day. Occasionally there's a sense of wonder or a feeling of peace while you're practicing, but there's also often just frustration and fidgeting.

The good news is that it actually doesn't matter. The physical structure of our brain is still changing slowly and incrementally as we practice, which reduces our stress levels and increases our ability to be present to our daily lives. I've been saying this throughout, but psychological and emotional fitness is just like physical fitness. The analogy extends here too. We don't generally go to the gym because we love being at the gym, or even in order to get good at being at the gym. We go to the gym to get fit, so our lives are healthier as a result.

Psychological and emotional fitness is just as important as physical health, especially if we want to give our children the most wonderful childhood that we can.

3. Making friends with your emotions

Whenever you think or you believe or you know,
you're a lot of other people:
but the moment you feel, you're nobody-but-yourself.

~ E E cummings

Let's not forget that the little emotions are the
great captains of our lives
and we obey them without realising it.

~ Vincent van Gogh

Whether we think we're the emotional type or not, emotions play an inescapable role in our parenting. We often think it's our children's emotions that are the difficult part of our lives, but it's actually our own emotions that make a much bigger contribution to our homes.

Most of us parent pretty well – or at least the way we want to – until we're triggered by something our children have or haven't done. Of course, there may be things we're not sure how to do – like potty training or managing screen time – but we talk to a friend or ask Dr Google and we figure it out. It's only when the 14-month-old next door is out of nappies and our three-year-old hasn't got the hang of the potty yet, or when no one else's teenagers seem to be as screen-addicted as ours, that we get triggered into an emotional response and often start to parent in ways we're not so proud of.

When these situations occur, we tend to move into one of two modes: either fight or flight (if we're triggered into red brain), or into a mode I call 'change, fix or solve' (if we slip into orange). This switch can happen so automatically that we often have no idea we've even had an emotion. It's only if we stop and notice that we feel the rising frustration or anxiety.

We need to start with kindness towards ourselves in terms of how our children trigger us. It really is a relationship like no other in our lives; it's as if there's an emotional umbilical cord between us. Our kids can make us feel so much reflected glory and so much reflected humiliation. Everything from their behaviour to their skills, talents and challenges affect us at a visceral level. When our children succeed at something, we get a hit of green-brain hormones, as if it's happening to us. Similarly, when our children struggle or fail at something, we often get a dump of red-brain hormones.

You've only got to wander around a sports field on a Saturday morning to see this in action. There's so much yelling at the one person we love the most in the world, amidst, of course, incredible excitement at a goal scored or elation over a win. It's not unbelievable competitiveness or huge ambition that drives this; it's a cascade of hormones. We all get this. Some people show it externally, while some don't, but we all feel it. The things our children do or don't do – from their development and their obedience, to their failures and successes – affect us more than almost anything in the world. This means it's an emotional rollercoaster to be a parent.

When I'm working with parents, they often tell me that their children know how to push all of their buttons with great expertise. It really does feel like that, but our children are far too involved in their own worlds to have the time or the headspace to have worked out specifically what triggers us.

Given that our children will trigger reactions in us on a regular basis, how we respond becomes the key difference between enjoying parenting or not. Before I came across mindful parenting, I tried lots of different parenting techniques to get through the day. The frustrating thing, for me, was that they all came with the words calm and consistent attached to them. It was the endless paradox. When I could do calm and consistent, I didn't really need techniques. When I needed something to help me through, I was not feeling remotely calm or able to be consistent. I now think that there is no calm and consistent parenting technique that we can stick to effectively when we have already moved into red brain. Those situations simply become a subtle battle for whose red brain, at that time, will be the more powerful.

The first step to shifting patterns of reactivity on our part, is to turn the spotlight – gently and kindly – on ourselves. We first need to begin to understand what emotions are, what they do to our body and our brain, and how to process them well.

WHAT ARE EMOTIONS?

As I mentioned in the last chapter, our brain works a bit like a radar so when we detect a threat or a reward, it releases a chemical message to let us know. Our emotions are the result of these chemicals travelling through the body. The word emotion itself refers to a motion of energy. The hormones that we've talked about already cause physical and chemical changes in our brain and body that scientists have various ways of measuring. They can track the levels of our hormones by measuring brain activity, heart rate, skin reactivity and even pupil dilation.

As we've touched on already, if we detect something rewarding, our brain releases serotonin, oxytocin and dopamine, and – naturally – we enjoy the sensation. The only downside is that we may struggle until we get more of that feeling.

If we detect a threat, cortisol and adrenaline kick in, but unless we're dealing with a genuine emergency we need a completely different response to resolve the situation effectively. If we don't, our responses from then on will be affected, both directly and indirectly, by having those hormones in our system.

Emotions are physical realities and we need to understand them, validate them and learn to regulate them, rather than try to ignore or prevent them. Understanding and regulating our emotions is known as emotional intelligence, and I believe it's almost impossible to enjoy parenting without it.

UNDERSTANDING OUR EMOTIONS

Humans experience four basic emotions. These are like umbrella categories within which all of our emotions fit. These emotions are happiness, sadness, anger and fear.

I often ask people which of these four emotions they associate with green brain. Happiness is, of course, the one most commonly mentioned.

Sometimes people think fear or sadness might possibly be felt in green brain, but never anger. The reality though is that having healthy access to all four is crucial to living in green.

The metaphor I use is that we have an emotion balloon inside us that has four openings or vents – one for each category of emotion. Just like our traffic light brain colours, the emotion balloon is a huge simplification of what is actually a complex reality, but it's still a helpful way to get a better understanding of how our emotions work.

You may not have come across the idea of learning to experience all of your emotions – including the difficult ones – in the endless amount of literature and resources dedicated to the pursuit of happiness. It's not generally a popular idea. However, access to all of our emotions is the way we're designed to function and to live with full vitality as human beings. The pursuit of happiness is, ironically, often its own undoing. When we avoid or shut down our other emotions, we also reduce our chances of sustainable happiness.

In some ways, we're at a huge advantage once we become parents. Even if you managed to limit your emotional range before having kids, it's unlikely you will be able to once they arrive. You will, no doubt, feel more joy, more fear, more anger and more sadness than at any other time in your life. Here's why we need all four emotions.

HAPPINESS

Happiness is the word we generally use to cover all of our positive feelings – from calm and peace, to joy and excitement, to love and pleasure, to a feeling of having meaning and purpose. Happiness often describes the good feelings we have as a natural response to external events in our lives that go our way. However, happiness is also linked to wellbeing, which reflects a deeper sense of feeling ok in the world and having a good relationship with ourselves. As we've mentioned, happiness tends to be associated with the brain-building and bond-promoting hormones dopamine, serotonin and oxytocin.

FEAR

Fear is the feeling of threat. It keeps us safe and stops us from making dangerous decisions. Fear warns us to pay attention if something doesn't feel safe. Fear is a message to avoid or be careful of something. It's anxiety or panic; it's a hit of adrenaline associated with what-ifs. Without the ability to feel fear we wouldn't have survived as a species.

Fear can also be a message that we've reached the edge of our natural comfort zone. It opens up the possibility of choosing to be brave and moving beyond our comfort zone. Fear is often misunderstood as a lack of courage, but without fear we can't actually be brave. Courage isn't the absence of fear; courage is fear 'walking', or fear in motion.

Throughout our lives we make constant choices about whether our feelings of fear are a message to be careful and move away from something – because it feels unsafe or we're not ready to take on that particular challenge – or to be brave and move towards whatever the situation is. So fear is a helpful emotion in order to work out healthy decisions in our lives.

Anxiety is a word that has become so associated with a mental health condition that it's easy to forget it's an emotion in the fear family. When we recognise the sensation of anxiety as an important message rather than an illness, we're more likely to be able to find ways to begin to understand it and work with it.

SADNESS

Sadness is the feeling of loss. It covers a huge spectrum of losses – from grief at one end of the spectrum, to the loss of a job, an opportunity, a friendship, or your child's nap at the other end. We need to be able to feel sadness in order to process well anything in our lives that feels like a loss. Sadness is an emotion that's often pushed down or replaced by anger, as if somehow to be mad – rather than sad – is a sign of strength.

The healthy response to your child dropping their daytime nap (assuming you enjoy the break), is to recognise what you've lost – probably time to yourself during the day, or an opportunity to get some stuff done without a little helper in tow. When we recognise the sadness we feel in this situation, as opposed to drifting towards frustration, we're much more likely to process and take on board the emotion and the event smoothly. We may even find an alternative to what we've lost.

The same is true of a failed job interview, a broken relationship or any other loss. Of course, we may be angry with the other person, be they an interviewer or an ex-partner. We might also be afraid that we won't get another opportunity or relationship like this one, but the primary emotion is loss, and this loss needs to be acknowledged and felt rather than ignored and carried with us into the future.

ANGER

Anger is the most misunderstood of the emotions. It's often thought of as an unhealthy emotion, or just as a cover-up for feelings of sadness or fear. It is fair to say it's often used to prevent us feeling our softer emotions – for instance we may blame others in reaction to something we're scared of, or feel frustrated at a loss or a disappointment. But healthy anger carries its own important message.

Anger is the emotion of injustice and is a natural response to someone pushing or crossing our boundaries. Anger is crucial to a healthy life, to our ability to put good boundaries in place, to say no and to stand up for others. In kindergarten our kids are taught to say, "Stop it, I don't like it" when they feel uncomfortable with the way someone is treating them. That's green-brain anger in action. My teenagers need access to their own healthy "no" as they explore life with more freedom, and away from the protection we could give them when they were younger.

Because of its negative connotations, I think anger needs some new, green-brain names. My favourites are calm definiteness, healthy boundaries, dignity, and justice.

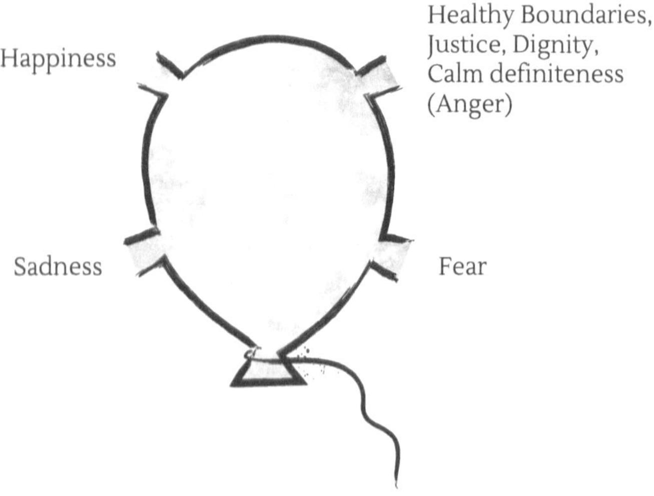

As parents, we need access to healthy anger. Our children cross our boundaries regularly and do things that are deeply unfair to others around them. They are scientists, testing the world around them and determining what are the physical, emotional, social and ethical limits to their world. And we are there to help them understand what is and isn't helpful. If we don't have the ability to get to anger in green, to protect the people in our homes from one another with calmness and kindness, it's likely that we'll regularly experience explosive anger, or feelings of helplessness and a loss of control. That's simply the fight-or-flight response that anger in red brain creates.

Now that we're clued into the four families of our emotions, the next thing is to understand how we handle each of these and the impact this has.

HOW WE HANDLE OUR EMOTIONS

There are three main ways that we deal with our emotions, and they are generally linked to our family of origin, our life experiences and our personality. We do respond to our emotions in all three ways depending on the situation, but we generally have a bias towards one of the three.

- We get stuck in them
- We suppress them
- We process them.

To help us understand these responses in action, let's come back to the balloon analogy.

GETTING STUCK IN OUR EMOTIONS

The first response we may have to an emotion is that we feel it and we find it hard to shake, so the emotion gets stuck. Even if we forget about how we're feeling for a while, a stuck emotion comes back repeatedly. This can feel like internal discomfort or a nagging sense of things not being quite right, or be more specifically related to an event that has affected us.

Maybe you got really upset with your kids and said things you wish you hadn't – you know those awful moments when you tell them the actual truth about how you're feeling towards them rather than swallowing hard and restraining yourself. Maybe you've never done it but I have, and I work with so many parents who then replay the words over and over, wishing time would go backwards and they could unsay what's been said.

If you are stuck with these tricky emotions, you might keep justifying it to yourself (anger in fight) or keep beating yourself up about it (anger in flight). It's a swing that many of us hop on, and it's one that rarely comes to a stop quickly.

Maybe, rather than having said things you regret, you're worried about how one of your children is doing (fear), and you're unable to feel calm until you know they're going to be ok. Perhaps you have a difficult deadline at work that's looming, and you're finding it difficult to relax until that project is done (again, fear). Or maybe someone said or did something thoughtless and you can't stop thinking about it and feeling a bit hopeless (sadness). It could also be something significant from the past that still triggers you when you're reminded of it. The way your mum or dad treated you, or a past relationship that didn't end well. Whether they're current situations that keep us stuck, or emotions not present constantly but which come back sharp and intense from time to time, this is what stuckness feels like.

If we get stuck in our emotions, we often live in an overactive state, with an uncomfortably tight emotional balloon. We experience heightened stress levels, irritability and low mood. We can be hard to live with as we have a lot of emotions that need to be processed and released, but often are just expressed and then repeated. It's common, if you're the stuck type, that you had at least one parent growing up who also got stuck in their emotions.

I'm mostly a 'stucky', which means although I suppress in certain situations I largely feel my emotions strongly and find them hard to shake. I get a knot in my stomach or a tight feeling in my chest when I think back to certain events or forward to what's ahead. I also tend to replay conversations, real or imagined, over and over in my mind. Rarely does all the revisiting or replaying move me forward or resolve anything; it just goes around and around. Sometimes time softens the blow, but not always.

The words 'sensitive' and 'over-sensitive' are often used for people who get stuck in their emotions. Neither word is particularly helpful when it comes to describing what's actually being experienced. Those of us who feel our emotions more strongly and often get stuck are also more likely to experience empathy for other people's emotions too. We tend to be the feelers in life. Other people's feelings matter to us, but we're also more vulnerable to the day-to-day effects of our own.

SUPPRESSING OUR EMOTIONS

The second response we can have to an emotion is to suppress it. We push it down into our subconscious, hoping that will be enough to get rid of it. In some ways, suppression is more confusing to us than getting stuck, because we really do believe we've dealt with our difficult feelings. In the example above, rather than ruminating on the words that spilled out of our mouths, we might feel that nothing much can be done, it's happened and its now in the past and we avoid those uncomfortable feelings and move on.

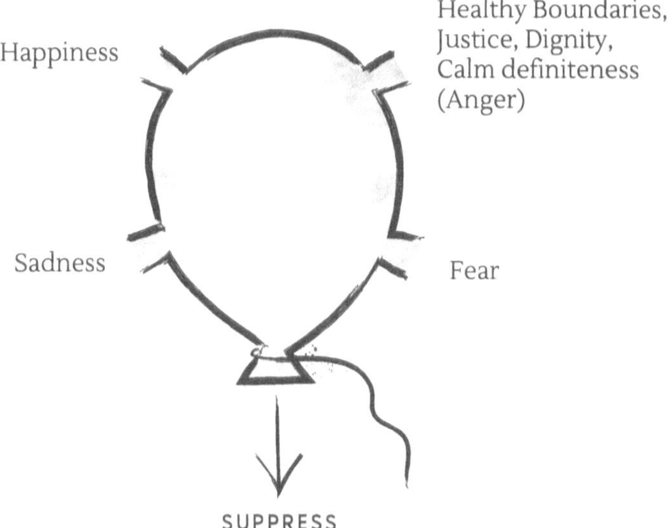

Suppressors can be easier to live with as they're often calmer people but over time the 'I'm fine', 'It is what it is', or 'It's all in the past', has a significant effect on our lives and relationships. Feelings always re-emerge from the subconscious – often in an indirect way – and the impact may be harder to handle.

In my experience of working with parents, suppression is commonly linked to living in orange brain. Suppression feels like a practical solution to inconvenient emotions, when the to-do list is extensive and there's not enough time to get through it all. Suppressors tend to struggle to see the validity of emotions in themselves or others. As with 'stuckies' above, often suppressors have had at least one parent growing up who also suppressed their emotions.

SUPPRESSION AND TIME

If you're pushing down or suppressing your emotions, you can generally do so for short, medium or long periods of time. Again, there's no hard-

and-fast rules with these timeframes, but here's what they tend to look like:

Short-term suppression is when we swap one emotion for another almost instantaneously. Imagine you're at the playground with your children. They may be a bit scratchy with each other. They're not sharing well, but so far no one is getting hurt and there's no one else there to see them, so you leave them to it. Then another family turns up. You rush in to discipline your kids and try to get them to behave better. The emotion you may think you're feeling is anger or frustration, because your kids crossed behavioural boundaries. But it's much more likely that what actually triggered you was embarrassment, which is in the fear category. In this case, you were experiencing fear of what the other family might think of you or your kids.

Why does this matter? Because the initial emotion was suppressed, the eventual emotion comes out in red – and parenting will be much harder as a result. When we become more aware of our emotions, we can deal with them as they come up and most importantly in the present. Even if we do decide to step in and do something now that someone's watching, we can see the funny side of what just happened to us, which keeps us greener and makes parenting so much easier.

Beyond instant reactions, short-term suppression refers to a day or a few days. Maybe you've had a hard day at work, but you're not comfortable admitting that you're overwhelmed by how much you have to do. You muddle along with your ever-expanding balloon. You get home feeling edgy. The kids want your attention and seem to have no idea that you need space to unwind. Your balloon starts to leak from the anger outlet, and you get increasingly disconnected, grumpy and resentful towards everyone.

Maybe you've been home with the kids all day and it's not been a good day. Your children haven't listened well, and the house is a mess, but you've managed to control your feelings. You haven't sold them, or even yelled at them – yet. You're exhausted from the effort and your balloon is tight. When your partner comes home and forgets to ask about your day, you feel resentful or tearful or you lose it.

Medium-term suppression covers things that have happened in the last few weeks or months and that are still clear in your memory. For example, your partner habitually forgets to put the rubbish out or clear up after themselves and, although you mention it in passing, you continue to do the jobs yourself and try not to think about it too much. When your partner complains that you've spent too much money that month, your suppressed emotions are triggered and out it all comes.

Or maybe you go for a job interview and the hours and the salary fit the needs of your family really well. You don't get the job, and you respond by suppressing your feelings of rejection or loss. 'It's fine, there are plenty more jobs out there', or 'Idiot, she should be sent on an interviewing course, I wouldn't work for her anyway.' That works for a while, until you see the person who got the job a few weeks later in the street, and you feel the full strength of your emotional response. None of your original emotions have been processed and you can feel it.

Long-term suppression is something we probably all have some idea about. We learn patterns in our childhood of how to manage our emotions – often according to how our parents dealt with theirs. This can mean that we may have certain emotions we're really uncomfortable feeling or expressing because they weren't encouraged in our home. If that's your experience, you may well have suppressed some emotions for a long time. As a result, you may view yourself and others in unhealthy ways.

Anger is a common one that families avoid. Some families are also dismissive of sadness and fear, or they think those emotions are appropriate only at a certain age, or for a particular gender, or only in specific circumstances. I had one client whose father used to say to her, "No blood, no tears." She learned from a very young age that the emotion of sadness was only acceptable if there was raw physical evidence to support it. In other families, fear is seen as weakness, instead of being a healthy emotion that is not only valid, but also here to tell us something important.

I have a close friend who I met when our eldest children started school together, more than ten years ago. She is one of the most balanced and joyful people I know. When she learnt about the four emotions, she had a moment of realisation. She discovered that anger, fear and happiness had all been ok in her family growing up, but not sadness. It was an emotion that she automatically suppressed. She had done so for years and, as a result, she felt the need to constantly cheer up her children and encourage them to be positive. Now she is able to validate her own sadness when she feels it and is also able to let her children feel theirs too. Not only are they all now more balanced, and, ironically, happier, but her job as a parent has reduced as a result of not feeling so much responsibility for her kids' feelings.

Every time we suppress an emotion, be it for a short time or a long time, it's a bit like putting pieces of dry kindling into our subconscious; we have no idea when a match will set it all alight. It may not necessarily be explosive, but our unprocessed emotions will keep trying to find their way back into our conscious mind, and back to our thoughts and feelings. Our unprocessed emotions often find expression in messy and confusing ways, either psychologically, physiologically or in our relationships.

In some cases, years of suppressing emotions can lead to issues with depressive feelings or anxiety, struggles with intimacy, difficulty knowing how to get your own needs met, and emotions that feel out of proportion to whatever the triggering situation may be.

Both those who get stuck and those who suppress can have a strong reaction to something relatively small, and for different reasons. For a stuck person, it tends to feel as if we're maybe a bit edgy and anxious until one final thing pushes us over the edge – even if that thing could be as simple as lost keys or a dying phone battery. For suppressors, there may have been no discernible sense of overwhelm, and strong reactions can seem to come out of nowhere. The subterranean pressure of suppression eventually becomes too much to sustain, and results in some form of strong and often surprising expression.

Before I move on to processing, one of the patterns I see regularly is one parent in a relationship who leans towards getting stuck in emotions and one who leans towards suppression. It can work well for a time, but at some point the differences become challenging for each partner to handle. For the suppressor the stuck partner can feel overwhelming and for the stuckie the suppressor can feel out of reach. In the blend of family life often the children are drawn towards one of these approaches, according to their own personality, and begin to develop a way of handling their emotions that is almost a copy of one of their parents. As neither approach is healthy or sustainable, we need a third way to respond to our emotions.

PROCESSING OUR EMOTIONS

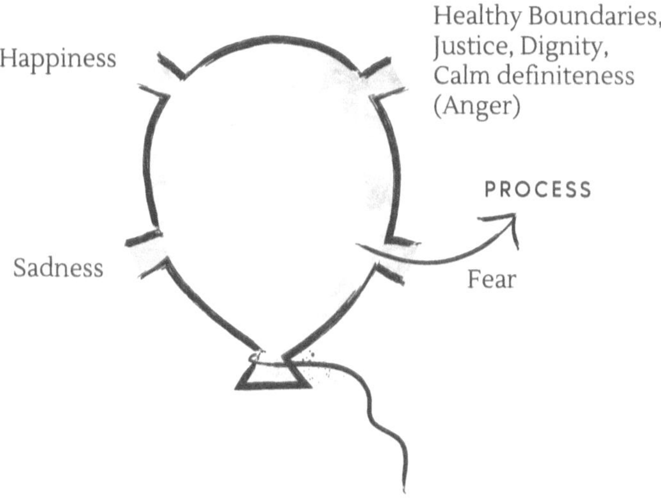

The third response to an emotion is to process it. Processing an emotion means that we experience our brain's chemical response to a situation, and we can let it out of the right vent. Our balloon fills up, we recognise what's happening, and we can let the energy go.

It sounds ideal, because it is. It's a process that happens naturally for most of us with happiness. Something good happens, serotonin is released into our body and we feel happiness. Our emotion balloon expands, and we grin or laugh, hug or dance, or we tell someone our good news. The balloon then releases the serotonin gently and our body returns to its normal levels.

With the three trickier emotions, processing doesn't tend to come as naturally – although some people find processing these emotions easier than others, depending on the emotional landscape of their upbringing. The result is that while our balloon is designed to have all four vents equally open, some of us have certain vents closed over and others a little overstretched. If you often lose your temper, are tearful or feel anxious, it doesn't mean you're processing that emotion well, it means you're probably stuck in the emotion and repeating it over and over. The balloon is unbalanced; that particular opening is too wide and one or more of the vents will be shut off a bit and you may struggle to feel other emotions. Your balloon may look something like this.

If any of the other emotion vents are either shut or stretched then happiness is almost always the casualty, though our lives can also be affected in other ways. Maybe you can feel and express anger, but the softer emotion of sadness is foreign to you, and so you struggle with intimacy. Maybe you experience ongoing anxiety and, while you choose to show happiness outwardly, you've shut off the emotion of anger, so you struggle to put good boundaries in place.

If you are a life-long suppressor, it may be hard to recognise yourself in some of these descriptions. But if you don't feel anything much at all, it's likely you've learnt – maybe when you were very young – that emotions weren't valuable. Your vents may be shut, and suppression is so habitual that you're unaware of it consciously. The telltale signs in this case may be a lack of joy and flashes of anger, or bouts of lowness or depression, as your body tries to cope with all the deeply hidden emotional chemistry you're holding on to.

Our children start out with a healthy balloon with all four vents open; they begin in perfect balance. Because we can be uncomfortable with the more challenging emotions, we often teach our kids – inadvertently – to hold some of their trickier emotions in. Sometimes our children then move to stuckness, which means they get totally hijacked by their emotions and express them in increasingly intense ways. Or they move to suppression, which for some means they try to stay composed, leading to sudden outbursts that can make them later feel ashamed or embarrassed. For other children who suppress, they really do learn to be stoic, and often become competitive or driven as this reduces the chances of feeling difficult emotions like failure.

We'll look at how to help our children with their emotional patterns in more detail in Chapter Five. For now, we're going to dive deeper into our own.

INSIGHT QUESTIONS - EMOTIONS

Draw your own emotion balloon, noting on it if you think any of your vents may be stretched or closed off. If you tend to get stuck in your emotions, draw a spiral. If you're more of a suppressor, indicate that with an arrow. It may be that you deal differently with different emotions or around different people – add that too.

Do you see any links between your balloon and how your parents dealt with their emotions?

Are there any emotions you may be inadvertently shutting off in your children?

PUTTING PROCESSING INTO PRACTICE

*"Between stimulus and response there is a space. In that space is our power
to choose our response. In that response lies our growth and our freedom."*

~ Victor Frankl, psychiatrist, author and Holocaust survivor

This quote is one of my favourites. It's one of the few I've ever learnt by
heart. I'm aware that comparing our situation as parents to Frankl's experience in Auschwitz could be misinterpreted. It's an impossible act to follow. But, at its core, is the idea that all of us can learn the skill of changing
our responses rather than trying to change the provocation.

I'm going to introduce you to a powerful mindfulness technique that
I use on a regular basis, both for myself and with the parents I work with.
It's a practical tool for processing our emotions and can be used in the
space between stimulus and response, so we don't get stuck or resort to
suppression.

Before we go through it, just in case you're tempted to skip the exercise and move on to the chapters that focus on your children, my experience has been that my relationship with my children has changed
significantly since I began to process my own emotions. I'm not totally
sure how much of it is that they're responding differently to the changes
in me, and how much of it is that I'm not so triggered by their behaviour.
Either way, you won't need to work nearly as hard with your children, if
you start with yourself.

CORE SKILL 2:
ACKNOWLEDGE, LINK, LET GO (ALL)

I've included a diagram here to start with, as it helps to envisage the process, and what's happening in our body and our brain during this exercise.

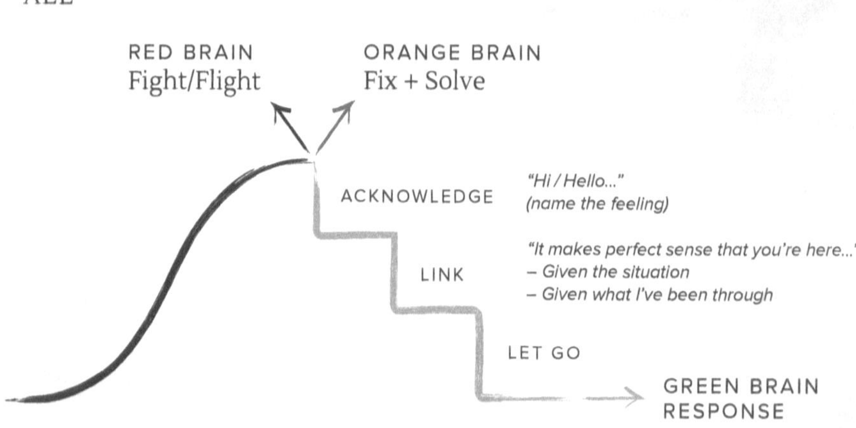

When we're processing a challenging emotion, we generally have a trickle or a burst of cortisol, which is represented here by the red arc. If we respond to whatever situation we're in from the top of the arc, we're led into further red-brain reactive thoughts and interactions or orange-brain attempts to fix and solve. The idea behind this practice – proposed by therapist Pauline Skeates – is that in order to help us get back to green, we can follow a simple three-step mindfulness process. The process helps us to pay attention with kindness to our emotions and regulate them well, instead of reacting from our red-brain state.[1]

A FOR 'ACKNOWLEDGE'

Think of a recent situation in which one of your children triggered a diffi-cult emotion in you. Take yourself back into that situation as fully as you can, and gently turn the spotlight away from your child or children and towards yourself.

First, pay mindful attention to your body and notice where you feel the emotion. It may be your muscles, in your chest, your head, or in your stomach. If you're on your own you can even say it out loud: "My muscles are tense", "I feel my heart racing", "I feel a bit nauseous", "It feels like my head is buzzing".

Now, move your focus from your body to your emotions. You may be feeling lots of things but see if you can identify the emotion that stands out the most. See if you can name it. Find a name that really feels like it fits. It could be anger, sadness or fear, or it could be a more specific name, like frustration, overwhelm, injustice, anxiety, helplessness, disappoint-ment, or rage. It could be that you were feeling out of control or taken for granted. Finding the best name really helps the process.

It may feel like frustration, but if you're screaming "It's not fair" inside, then it's probably injustice. It may feel like anger, but if you're shaking then rage may be a more helpful word. Once you've found the best name, you need to say hello to the emotion.

"Hi/Hello... " (name the emotion)

This is the acknowledgement part and it can feel odd at first, howev-er our brain can't process anything it hasn't first acknowledged. Saying 'Hello' is a simple way of doing that. It also places the emotion outside yourself, so it's just something you're experiencing. I encourage people to imagine the emotion has turned up at the door and they're just ac-knowledging its arrival.

L FOR 'LINK'

This is a crucial piece that's often missed in emotion-processing techniques. Acknowledging the emotion is not enough for our brain to process it fully; we also need to validate or make sense of the emotion. If you notice you're angry and count to ten, it can be helpful in the moment – but because emotions are messages, this style of handling difficult emotions leads to suppression rather than processing, since we're still not listening to why the emotion is there. The link sounds like this:

> "Hi... (name the emotion) ... It makes perfect
> sense that you're here, given the situation."

Once you've said these words to yourself, stop and pay attention to the effect they have on you. Notice if there's any resistance. Say the words again: "It makes perfect sense, given the situation". There may be shifts in your body, your thoughts or your emotions when you say this. You may be reminded of the events leading up to the trigger, or other reasons why this emotion is so valid. In doing so, you're paying attention (with curiosity) to your emotion. Be open to anything that you notice.

A lot of the parents I work with are surprised at the impact that the linking words "It makes perfect sense" have almost immediately. Their brain experiences empathy and relaxes, and some of the cortisol starts to come out of the balloon immediately. The emotion makes sense, and that can be enough to let go of it and get back to green.

It's important to understand we're not making sense of behaviour here, whatever it may have been at the time; we're making sense of the emotion. We're working in the space between the stimulus and the response.

In many situations our emotions don't seem to make sense, even given the situation. In some cases, they can seem out of proportion to the trigger. We then need a deeper step in the linking process, which sounds like this:

> "Hi... (same emotion as before) ... It makes perfect sense you're here given what I've gone through" or "given my childhood".

All our emotions make perfect sense given our childhood, our experiences, our personality, our birth order, our gender, our day, our week, or our year, plus the current trigger. There is no such thing as over-sensitive or over-reactive.

Once you've said, "It makes perfect sense given what I've gone through", notice anything that comes to your mind. Don't dismiss anything, but also try not to analyse what comes up for you. You're allowing things to bubble up from deep in your conscious or even your subconscious mind. These could be memories, people, events, ideas, core beliefs about yourself and others. You want all the information that your intuition can provide so that you can begin to recognise why this emotion makes perfect sense.

It can be a difficult distinction to make, but you are not just making cognitive sense of your emotion — this is not just about getting a moment of understanding. You are also gently offering yourself empathy for those past experiences and what they meant to you. Often the act of making sense feels like an acceptance in the body — a relaxation of the shoulders, or an expelling of air.

The kinds of common links that clients of mine have discovered are a fear of failure, a need for control or perfection, a desire to please authority figures, a feeling of never being good enough, a lack of opportunity, a role change in which they became the caregiver as a child, or an experience of bullying or disempowerment.

It takes a bit of practice, but, if you take your emotions seriously, they will start to emerge from your subconscious. In doing so, you will probably find out all sorts of things about yourself that you haven't paid attention to before.

The two links – current and past – are powerful for making sense of why you had a rush of cortisol that led to whatever behaviours you exhibited as a result of being triggered. Now you're ready for the last step.

L FOR 'LET IT GO'

Once you have named the emotion and linked it, your brain is ready to let it go from the balloon.

Place one hand on your chest and one hand on your stomach and take a deep breath. As you breathe out, let the emotion go. Take another deep breath and do the same again. And a third deep breath and let it go again.

The letting go part of this process can be helped by picturing the emotion leaving your imaginary balloon – you sense it quite literally being breathed out. It doesn't need to be a forceful action; it's more like a feeling of being held and understood, so your body relaxes and exhales, as you offer yourself empathy and validation.

Gently placing your hands on your body triggers that much-loved oxytocin in your brain, indicating that the cortisol is no longer needed, which also helps your brain relax. And the louder you breathe out, the more your brain connects to the idea that the emotion is leaving.

Once you've taken your three deep breaths, wait a few seconds longer and notice how you feel now. What are you aware of in these moments?

Finally, ask yourself: "What would help in this situation?"
Processing your emotion may be all that's needed, especially if it's your

past that's been triggered more so than the present situation. If the situation is over, then you may just notice possible responses you weren't able to access at the time, and you could next time. Often some action can still be taken – and the good news is that any action from here will now come from a green-brain state and will be far more effective.

Some emotions are processed relatively quickly, and ALL might only be needed once. Other emotions take longer, depending on how far back into your story they go, and you may need to repeat this exercise often. Similarly, if the emotion makes sense in the current situation, you can often let it go more easily than if it needs the second part of the link. Finding the deeper links has a greater long-term impact on your life, however.

COMMITTING TO YOUR PRACTICE

In the previous exercise, I have gone through how the practice works in detail: noticing what you're feeling with every fibre of your being, and how that emotion can shift as you gently make sense of it and let it go. The full, in-depth version requires a little time set aside to do it. However, these steps can be made to fit into the time that you have.

The shorter version goes like this:

THREE STEPS:

- Acknowledge: name your emotion
- Link: validate it
- Let go: breathe it out

It can sound as simple as: "Hi feeling of hopelessness (rage/anxiety etc), I know it makes perfect sense you're here given... (name the situation)... I let it go."

If you get stuck on the link, it still works to say, "I know it makes sense even if I haven't worked it out yet." Somewhere in the combination of your day, your personality, your life story and those many other ingredients, this emotion does make sense. You can commit to the process of exploring the link at another time, or you can leave it knowing it makes sense regardless of whether you've found the link or not. If an emotion trips you up regularly, however, finding the link is really worth doing, as it will reduce your reactivity to those events or triggers, either completely – or at least significantly – over time.

You can use ALL after you've experienced an emotion, as in the exercise above. You can also preempt situations by using it beforehand, if there are scenarios that you find yourself tripping up on repeatedly. With a little practice, you can even use the simplified version during an emotion. You don't need all the fine details, you just dive right in, name the emotion, validate it and let it go.

Committing to mindfully processing your emotions, by using ALL regularly, is key to developing the technique so that it comes easily. We're already likely to be dealing with cortisol and adrenaline from the emotion itself, so if the technique feels familiar and we feel skilled at it, we're better equipped to use it when we need it.

When I first started working with ALL, I used it not just daily, but many times a day. My stuck emotions began to shift more and more quickly, and I could almost feel the elasticity of my balloon as it filled and reduced. It sounds exhausting but, compared to feeling tense a lot of the time, it was a whole lot better. I could feel how healthy it was to notice when I was disappointed with the kids, when I felt all the housework I did was unfair, when I was afraid we didn't have enough money, or when I couldn't believe they were fighting again. Some of my emotions made sense just in the current situation, while some of them were linked to experiences from my childhood. The latter were the more powerful ones in terms of reducing my reactivity levels and increasing my mindful kindness towards myself.

I even used ALL pre-emptively during what was then still my morning carnage. I learnt to whizz around the house, saying under my breath, "Hi feeling of frustration. It makes perfect sense; no one is getting ready. Let it go...". "Hi feeling of frustration. It makes perfect sense; we're running late. Let it go...". It did make sense that getting five of them out the door on time wasn't easy, and it even made me laugh a little as I could feel the cortisol reducing, as I processed my feelings. The more powerful effect was that, after doing my ALL, my voice was calmer and more definite. I was less reactive and my children got ready with less stress and ultimately much more quickly.

EMOTION PROCESSING ENABLES BETTER PROBLEM SOLVING

Before we move on, I want to make it clear that processing emotions doesn't mean we ignore problems. It simply means we tackle those problems while we're in green brain as much as possible, rather than red or orange brain. I still had to parent the kids when I felt like giving up. I still had to have conversations about whose jobs were whose. I still had to budget. I still had to help my children sort out their disagreements. But, as I did these things, my tone began to change. My empathy for myself and for them grew, and I was able to take responsibility for what was mine and recognise what wasn't. What had previously been battlegrounds became conversations, negotiations and problem-solving exercises.

I'll look in greater detail at how to set mindful boundaries for our children around their difficult behaviours in Chapter Five, but the first step is that we need to be in green brain to do it effectively. In most situations, getting to green brain requires us to process our own emotions as we dive into them.

HOW I USE ACKNOWLEDGE, LINK, LET GO

I was watching a dance rehearsal in the school hall one afternoon. Two of my girls were on stage and two were watching. They were all happy and I was enjoying not having to do anything. I knew it was getting late, so I told the two watchers we needed to go soon. They complained and I decided to give them an extra half hour as long as they promised to leave calmly without a fuss when it was really time to go. (By the way, this is a terrible idea – don't ever do it!) Of course, my children agreed and, of course, they didn't mean it.

When it came time to leave, I ended up dragging two very resistant girls through the hall in front of everyone. We made it to the car, I shut the door and I let rip. I was so angry that, when I got home, I handed them over to my partner and flung myself down on my bed, knowing that my career as a mindful parenting coach was over.

When the mist cleared, I remembered I had my ALL technique. I tentatively started with the name. *Frustration?* No. Definitely *rage*. Such an outburst made no real sense given the situation, which was just two little girls reluctant to leave somewhere fun. It was annoying. But rage-producing? Not so much. So, I moved on to part two. As I sat there, I noticed an old but familiar feeling creep over me. I sat with it a moment and realised it was best described as the feeling of being in a no-win situation. I stayed a little longer with the feeling and it took me back to my childhood. As a child I was under a certain pressure to please my mum, who was prone to anxiety and tearfulness. I vacillated between compliance – which helped her but not me – and rebellion – which helped me, but not her. I felt trapped and angry by being in a no-win situation.

Somehow the experience in the theatre had triggered that same old feeling of rage at being in a no-win situation. Nothing I could have done would have made that situation better. It made so much sense that my reaction was the rage of my seven-year-old self, and not really current at all. It also made sense of so many times in my parenting when I had over-reacted (as it's so often called) – given that parenting is often one long series of no-win situations.

I can honestly say I felt a wave of empathy wash over me as I thought about my childhood. I'm sure it was helped by the fact that my parents are now fully supportive of whatever decisions I make in my life. But emotions have a long history; they stay in our body and in our subconscious; they're a big part of our present reality. I let it go, and this particular emotion has rarely returned. No-wins are just that. Normal for parents, and now disconnected from my childhood, so that link has been processed.

Now I just work with, "Hi frustration; it makes perfect sense you're here: five kids all want different music in the car and that's just another no-win situation."

4. Connection: the magic ingredient

Children have never been very good at listening to their elders
but they have never failed to imitate them.

~ James Baldwin

Love consists in leaving the loved one space to be themselves while
providing the security within which that self may flourish.

~ Raine Maria Rilke

Learning about how our brain and our emotions work is the best place to start if we want to have a relationship with our children that enables them to thrive. Children have the best chance of developing to their fullest potential when they grow up around green-brained adults, and experience lots of different emotions in a safe environment where the adults in charge know how to process their own emotions and are comfortable with other people expressing theirs.

However, there are also things we can learn more directly about how our children are uniquely designed. Let's start with two of the most important pieces of information you will ever need to know about your children.

YOUR CHILDREN ARE BORN WIRED TO THRIVE

The first is that our children are not born neutral; they're born with the capacity to thrive and to flourish in a healthy way. They are born with everything they need to meet their full potential as human beings. Developmental psychologist Dr Gordon Neufeld has a great list of the incredible characteristics that our children have when they arrive – or that, given the right conditions, will naturally emerge in them.[1]

Your children are born:

- with a sense of agency and responsibility;
- full of vitality – not easily bored;
- with venturing forth energy;
- full of interests and curiosity;
- with a good relationship with themselves;
- able to recover from trauma;
- considerate and well-tempered;
- able to solve problems;
- resilient and resourceful;
- able to benefit from adversity.

These are just some of the characteristics on the list and I had three responses when I first read them.

The first was, *what happened to my children?* Some days mine don't seem to have any of these characteristics. Does that mean I got the only children in the universe with different wiring?

The second was that I'd be so proud if my kids turned out like this, despite the fact that none of the attributes listed describe what we usually think of in terms of success. There's no mention of intelligence, of salary, of what car they'll drive, of how many medals they'll win or exams they'll pass. There's also no guarantee of a consistently happy life; thriving involves being able to bounce back from adversity and recover from trauma.

The third response I had to this list of traits was that if they have all these things already in them, what do they need from me? I thought that it was my job to help them develop these things.

This brings me to the second most important thing we need to know about our children. Once their basic needs for food, shelter and safety are met, they only need one condition for their brain to thrive in all of the incredible ways that Dr Neufeld lists. They need connection.

THE CONDITION OUR CHILDREN REALLY NEED: CONNECTION

Developmental science shows that a safe, strong connection – often called an attachment relationship – with one caring adult is the main condition that enables all the amazing characteristics that our children have within them to develop. [2]

It turns out that, we're more like the gardener than the carpenter or the sculptor. It's a totally different role. Who our children are – or in this analogy, what type of plant they are – is out of our hands. Our children arrived already as they are, and they will only ever be either a healthy or an unhealthy version of themselves. Trying to design our children so they're how we'd like them to be is as pointless as trying to turn a tomato into a cucumber.

Instead, like a gardener, we offer our children the best conditions we can to help them grow to their full potential. We make sure that the soil is well-watered and healthy. We enable them to access as much sunlight as we can, although even that is often out of our hands. When we think about it this way, it's a much less complicated – and also far less intrusive – role than I had understood parenting to be.

This idea means that we can start with relaxing our more stressful ideas about what our children need in terms of stimulation, adventure, opportunities, resources and anything else we might have been persuaded will make a difference to how well they will do in life. Connection is the key to our children living the richest lives they possibly can and, to continue the metaphor, to being the strongest, healthiest and most abundant plant they could possibly be.

WHY CONNECTION?

For a young mammal in the wild, connection is essential to survival. When they get separated from the adult mammal, there is a significant risk of danger. For a human child the response is the same. Every time they feel disconnection, their brain automatically responds by triggering stress – until they feel connected again. Connection for our children isn't just about us being there physically; it's also about emotional or psychological connection. The need for this full gamut of connection stays true for our children well beyond the age that their survival relies on us being physically close.

A WORD ABOUT LOVE

You might be surprised that I use the word 'connection' rather than 'love' as the main condition our kids need to grow and develop to their fullest potential. The reason is that many children grow up with parents who love them deeply, but don't connect with them very well. Unfortunately, this sort of relationship doesn't enable children to fully flourish.

Many of you reading this book know your parents loved you, but they may not have been emotionally present with, or for, you. A lot of things can be done or said in the name of love that are much less likely when we use the word connection. Connection requires being together in some way, with a child really sensing that togetherness, to make it work. When we invest in connection with our children, we can see it working – not by the successful individuals we turn out, but by the quality of the relationship we share together.

THE WAYS WE DISCONNECT

Before I share some practical tools to help you foster a deeper and more mindful connection with your kids, I first want to look at the ways our children experience separation or disconnection. This understanding sets the context for connection, which is often quite a natural state when we remove some of the obstacles that disconnection can cause. Some things we do all the time without thinking can cause disconnection. Some of these are things we choose; some are reactions. Other disconnections we can do nothing about. However, there are some that we can reduce, and some that we can change. Let's take a closer look.

I find it helpful to think of separation in three categories:

PHYSICAL DISCONNECTION

Most physical separations feel quite natural or are simply unavoidable. We go to work; our children go to school or childcare. They do activities after school, and we all go to bed every night. Yes, even bedtime can feel like a separation for some children. Maybe your children only live with you every other week, or during the weekends.

Some children find these physical separations easy; they feel secure in their connection with us regardless of whether we are physically nearby or not. Other children find physical separation much harder. For these children, the moment of separation can be a tricky transition, or the time apart may be hard for them to handle.

I have identical twins – a split egg and as close as you can get to the same environment growing up. When school started, one separated happily and was far more excited to meet new friends than hang out with me. The other one wanted to stay by my side until the very last minute, and then wanted 'the longest cuddle in the world', which was still followed by real distress for a few minutes when I left.

Both of these responses can be perfectly healthy, and are simply a reflection of a child's personality, age and stage, or their experiences of that particular morning. If your child is struggling to let you go, they may just be looking for reassurance that, although you may be separating physically, your overall connection isn't changing at all.

The challenge with this, as you might imagine, is that when we respond with frustration, try to apply logic, or dish out ultimatums, we're actually confirming our child's fear that they aren't safely connected to us. "Can't you see your sister is fine?", "But you really like your teacher", or "That's enough now" rarely work. If a child is reacting to physical separation then we are not answering their fundamental question, which is 'Are we still connected when you go?'

If our children could say, "Dad, I'm feeling nervous about you leaving me this morning, can you help?" it would be so much easier. But this is all completely subconscious for them. They just feel scared, or resistant, or are unsettled because their socks are itchy. When we react by trying to speed up the process of separating, we often find our children's behaviour ramps up and we have a cling-on attached to our legs.

I'm going to look at strategies for helping us to deal with physical separation later in the chapter, but a simple understanding of what might be going on for your child may already help you to adapt your response.

ACTION-BASED DISCONNECTION

Our action-based separations are subtler than our physical ones, as we're usually in the same space at the time that we do them. Phone calls, texting, being on the computer, chatting to someone else, distracted interactions when we're not really listening, doing household jobs when we're just feeling generally stressed, or simply in orange brain – these can all feel like separations to our children.

Have you ever noticed how your child can be playing happily but they suddenly need your attention the minute you pick up the phone? Or maybe you've been at the playground and they're fine until your friend arrives with a coffee, and they choose that moment to come running over, unable to play a moment longer until you push them on the swing. It can also happen commonly with siblings. We show one child some affection and another child discovers they urgently need a cuddle.

Without an understanding of their need for connection, these moments can feel perverse, planned or just plain ridiculous. But when you think about it in the context of connection, it suddenly all makes sense. We may not have been interacting with them beforehand, but we were potentially available. When we become unavailable, or our attention is somewhere else (especially if it is focused on someone else), they often need to come and check in with us. And because this action-based disconnection can often trigger them into red brain, that checking in can look like anything from persistent interruptions to a full-blown tantrum.

It's often called attention-seeking. But to their minds they are genuinely mitigating some kind of threat, so I call it 'connection-checking', even though the checking can be pretty intense.

Our children's need for connection doesn't mean that we can't chat with our friends, talk on the phone, or shower a different child with all the love in the world. It's healthy for our children to have to work through the reality that our connection with them is rock solid even when we're not paying them attention. There are lots of different ways to help them do that and we will look at some of these techniques later in this chapter. For now, I will give you just a few examples that relate to the scenarios we've imagined here.

In the playground, a cuddle and an invitation to stay nearby while we chat to a friend is often enough to send them trotting off happily. They soon discover just how boring adult conversation is. This may not work every time, but it has more chance than when we tell our children off for being rude and for interrupting. The latter response will make them stay longer, ramp up their interruptions, or leave with their tail between their legs. If they leave like that, they will be much more vulnerable to a meltdown if they fall, or to having a fractious interaction with another child, which started because they're feeling disconnected to us.

At school drop-off, letting our child know we'd love to spend the day with them (and sounding like we mean it) can ease the transition. It sounds counterintuitive, but our children are surprisingly resilient when the boundary (which is, in this case staying at school) isn't up for discussion and we're still reinforcing our connection with them. Of course, they may still need to be prised away from us when the bell goes, but at least we'll be in green brain when that happens. Once they've recovered, they'll know that connection is still securely there.

With siblings vying for connection, easy phrases like "You'd love a cuddle too, I can't wait" remind your child that there's plenty to go round, but the first cuddle is not going to be cut short.

And yet, there are no magic bullets and our kids may still not respond well to these physical or action-based disconnections. At a day-to-day level, when we're busy, and especially if we're in orange brain, we can often be quite forbidding when our children feel the need for connection. As we whizz around the house or the supermarket focused on what we need to do, our children sense they're not as important as our jobs, and often behave in ways that appear demanding. We then get impatient, or we slip in a pointed learning lesson about 'good' behaviour or waiting politely, neither of which a child sensing disconnection can do. And, of course, we ramp up their feelings of separateness with our response to them. The cycle continues.

One of the most common scenarios I see with the parents I work with starts with both parent and child wanting valid and valuable things: jobs completed (for the parent) and connection (for the child). As these two desires collide, the result is disconnection. Given connection is our children's lifeblood, we often see really tricky behaviours coming from kids in busy orange-brained homes.

When we start with a connection-based approach (which you'll see how to create soon) normal family life – including all those unavoidable tasks we need to do – is still possible with a green-brain connection intact.

For teenagers, or those approaching the teen years, the need for connection is often more subtle, although just as strong. They need interaction and interest in their lives that's open-ended, curious and without judgment. It can be as simple as showing interest in their friendships, their food preferences, their screen lives or their decisions, with a genuine desire to learn about them rather than to judge them in any way. Many teenagers turn to their peer group for their deepest connection, not because that's what works best for their brain development, but because – as parents – we're unsure how to connect. We start to approach our teens with suspicion, concern or lists of instructions.

I worked with one dad whose teenage son was in trouble with the police, and he told me he had thought his job was done when his children turned 13. He believed that his children needed food and shelter and some guidance here and there, but that their emotional needs would be met by their friends. It's a common misconception, because it's often what our teenagers seem to want, and maybe it's something we experienced ourselves as teens to a greater or lesser extent.

Adolescence is a crucial time for our children to have their safest and deepest connection at home. This connection then allows them to really spread their wings and thrive in their relationships outside of their family. The amount of time we spend with them may still be far less than the time they spend with their friends, but having a strong and healthy connection at home enables them to navigate the often unpredictable world of adolescent relationships with more confidence, creativity and resilience.

REACTION-BASED DISCONNECTION

Lastly, before we move onto more of the practical strategies for building connection, I want to look at the final way that we disconnect. Reaction-based separations are quite different to the other two types of disconnection. Unlike physical and action-based separations – which may or may not make our children feel disconnected from us depending on their personality or just depending on the day – our reactions always cause emotional separation.

When we react in red brain to our children, it's generally because we're feeling under threat. We all tend to have our own repertoire of reactions, depending on whether we tend towards fight or flight. In fight we may yell and shout, try to reassert control, snap, threaten or we dole out consequences. In flight we become more passive-aggressive. We go silent and sulk, we sigh and give in, we throw out rhetorical questions like, "What were you thinking?" or plead with them for some obedience.

In response to our red-brain reactions, our children's brains also go straight to red. No matter how justified we may be, or how well-meaning our intentions – even how calm we try to be – if our brain is in red, our tone will give us away. And if a child senses red, they can only respond by going into red themselves; they have no option on that.

One of my children is extremely attuned to tone, and even when I think I got my words out in green, she knows. She'll tell me I'm shouting, when I know I'm not. What she's really saying is that it was a cross sound, so it's sounding loud in her head and heart, and she's always right.

OUR CHILD'S RESPONSE TO DISCONNECT

When our children feel disconnected – whether it's in response to a physical, action or reaction-based separation – the natural characteristics they're developing like resilience, vitality and responsibilty all pause for a while. Instead, because they are triggered into red brain, their energy gets diverted to the fight or flight response. It generally takes a moment of reconnection to get their brain back to healthy development.

Understanding this finally helped me see why there have been seasons in our home when few of the natural attributes that my children were apparently born with were thriving. For a number of years, I was regularly in a red- or orange-brain state and, as a result, my children were in fight-or-flight mode much of that time. They were unable to develop their natural problem-solving capacity, their resourcefulness and their curiosity.

A child in fight mode is easy to see. They're noisy, messy and often physical. They persist in trying to reconnect, getting attention any way they can. They may resort to hurting siblings, refusing to do anything we ask, become bossy and prescriptive or find it impossible to recover when they're upset or disappointed.

A child in flight mode is less easy to spot. They're often easier to handle, as they grab tightly onto the possibility of connection when they feel disconnected. They'll do what we say, even offering to be helpful, or behaving well and then wanting to be noticed and praised. But the disconnect they're experiencing often shows in indirect ways. Behaviours as diverse as bed-wetting, helplessness, anxiety, low self-esteem, difficulty taking risks and sudden emotional outbursts can all be related to a flight child who is trying to function in red without causing any trouble.

One client I worked with was struggling to handle her three-year-old daughter, who was showing both fight and flight tendencies. She was having a lot of tantrums, but one of her most disconcerting behaviours was that she would follow her mum down the corridor saying repeatedly "I love you Mummy". It sounds innocent enough, but her mum knew it didn't feel right. There had recently been a new baby in the family, and as we talked about what her daughter might be feeling, her mum felt she had started to expect more mature behaviours from her little girl since the birth of the baby. She realised it was possible that her daughter felt that as a loss of connection. She made a conscious decision to intentionally play more with her daughter and treat her as a three-year-old again, and not as the older sister. Over the next few weeks the girl stopped offering her love, and her tantrums became less and less frequent.

I know that stories like this can be hard. Our first response might be, 'But there's just no time when there's a new baby to focus on connection with another child.' It makes perfect sense to feel that way, but the time it takes to handle a disconnected child is so much more than the time it takes to invest in connection, so it's really the far easier route.

Not all of our children's difficult behaviours are linked to disconnection. They may just be exploring the world and pushing boundaries. We will talk a lot more about boundaries in the next chapter, but the behaviours of a well-connected child who is simply pushing boundaries and a child who's responding to disconnection can look the same in the moment. It can be difficult to figure out. Either way, connection is a great place to start. If it is a disconnection problem, the challenges dissolve over time with increased connection. If it's a boundary issue, it's much easier to set boundaries when we're well connected.

A WORD ABOUT PARENTAL GUILT

I know from running parenting courses for many years now that some of you will have jumped straight from 'Mmmm interesting' to parental guilt. It's a delicate area when we're learning new things and, in the process, discovering areas of our lives that we may have been doing in unhelpful ways. It's even more sensitive when we're talking about our children and their brain development, as arguably they are the people we most desperately want to get it right with.

I see a lot of clients who start to wilt when they discover how often they separate or disconnect from their children, and that some of the behaviours they're seeing from their children could be as a result of that disconnection. My job is to remind them that:

- The brain rewires with focused and directed attention, and our children's brains are in such a stage of dynamic growth that they rewire even more quickly. This means that any repeated change towards connection will rewire our children's brains relatively quickly, and we'll see more of their natural potential grow.
- Practicing our own mindfulness, in terms of daily exercises as well as processing our own emotions, means that we can offer ourselves kind and curious attention in each moment. And that's an environment in which guilt can't survive for long.

Guilt doesn't help us to be creative. By now you can understand why. Guilt simply puts us into red brain, where we can't learn or grow. When we get back to green brain, guilt transforms into insight, and then we can explore new ideas and where these can take us.

INSIGHT QUESTIONS - DISCONNECTION

Take a moment to write down what regular separations your children experience in each of the three categories. Focus especially on the ones you think they may be experiencing as disconnection.

PHYSICAL

ACTIONS

REACTIONS

Some of these disconnections are unavoidable, but write down one area in which you think you could reduce the experience of disconnection this week.

Write down one area that you would like to reduce that may take a little longer to tackle.

CORE SKILL 3:
UNCONDITIONAL CONNECTION

THE ART OF MINDFUL CONNECTION – THE BOX AND THE HEART

We can't change the fact that we all disconnect from our children regularly, and that's simply a part of life. Adjusting some areas so our kids experience less disconnection, however, gives us a head start. While genuine connection can emerge naturally, there are also ways that we can strengthen it. The heart and the box is a simple idea to help us do this, as we need to look at both the connector – the box – as well as the connection itself – the heart, or our relationship.

THE BOX

In the parent/child relationship, the child is the recipient and not the provider – or even an equal player – when it comes to connection. As parents, we're the ones offering the secure connection, which means we need to have a safe and secure base of our own and not be reliant on how our children are doing, or whether they seem to be reciprocating the connection or not. The box then, in this diagram, represents our secure base.

The box is about us as people, not just as parents. This box is our relationship with ourselves and our own green-brain life. If our box is solid and robust, our children can explore who they really are with more freedom, including their independence, their curiosities, their anger and so many other things that they need to discover about themselves, through trial and error, in order to grow up.

If our own box is shaky, then we can't offer our children that freedom, since they're then drawn in to trying to work out how to have a solid and reliable connection to a less-than-reliable parent. That's when things get messy.

Depending on the child, they will over time either withdraw from the connection into rebellion, or they will take on more of a compliant or 'good child' role to keep the peace or live up to our expectations. The latter response - the flight mode child - might seem preferable, but actually neither role promotes healthy brain growth in our children. So how we feel about ourselves, how healthy our own box is, will have a direct impact on how our children will feel about themselves.

Recognising that the system works this way can elicit feelings of guilt in us, but it's actually really good news. If we could stay living in red or orange brain ourselves – experiencing stressful and self-critical thinking, or run off our feet with all the things we have to do – and still have our children grow up to be strong and healthy, there would be far less motivation for us to change.

When I'm talking to parents, I often use words like *pilot, gardener, compass, role-model, anchor, guide* and even *cathedral* [3] as metaphors to help them understand the dynamic of the connection relationship, since they're a better reflection of the relationship we have with our children than that of friend, at one end of the spectrum, or sculptor at the other end. They all point in different ways to how we care for and relate to our kids from a respectful distance.

One of my clients was discussing with me the difficulties she was having with her two teenagers, and we started to explore some of these ideas about her role as a parent to see what she resonated with. When we reached the word 'cathedral' she started crying, before she then started grinning. It was just a word, but when I asked her about her reaction, she said it cut through all the ideas whizzing around her head about what she should and shouldn't be doing. The idea of a cathedral gave her the feeling of unintrusive but vast safety, which is a metaphor that she has hung onto.

That may not be the best word for you; you'll have your own word or words that better reflect the kind of relationship you have and would like with your children. Thinking about the relationship in different terms gently moves us away from micro-managing our children, and helps us to instead step back and focus on what sort of environment we want to create for them and what role we play in their lives.

If you think back to your own childhood, you may remember some events that were important to you. Your most immediate response is likely to be an abstract one though, related to the atmosphere you grew up in. You may feel safe, warm, significant, known, connected, or loved. Or you might feel cautious, resistant, judged, lonely, numb, or afraid. Your response relates to the box you were offered and how it felt to be connected to, and immersed in, the atmosphere of the adult or adults in your home.

THE 'MY SHIT' BOX

Given that we're all a work-in-progress, I think we need to add another box. It can be helpful to keep some things out of our relationship with our kids, even though they may still be part of our lives. This is not about pretending; in fact, it's great for our children to see that we're human and that we struggle sometimes. This suggestion is simply about making sure they're not on the receiving end of the expectations we have of them that come from our own struggles. This box can have a variety of names, so choose what works for you. It could be 'my stuff' or 'my work-in-progress' box. I find the more confronting language helpful, but it's not for everyone.

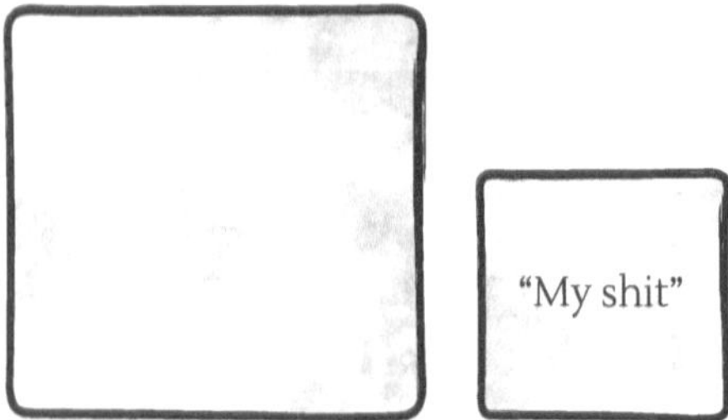

All of us have expectations, dreams and fears for our kids that are a direct result of our own triggers. Unless we become aware of them, we're likely to end up trying to sculpt our children around them.

We all have a story, and we all have fears. Those fears are often the driving force behind our need for our children to do well or be safe. It could be a need to look good in public, or to not fail at anything. It could be a desire to keep our kids safe from unhappy experiences we had ourselves. It could be that we struggled in a certain area and we can't bear them to, or that we were good at something and we can't imagine our children's lives without it.

There's a lot of heavy-handed parenting that clearly has little to do with connected love and everything to do with the parent's own story. If we have a story of rejection, or of being bullied ourselves, then we might become pushy when our kids struggle to make friends. If we judge our kids for how they look, it says more about our own body image than their appearance. If we need them to be good at everything, it says more about our own sense of not feeling good enough ourselves.

One of my least favourite phrases is 'as long as they try their best'. It leaves little room for failure and much less room for real passion in areas they're naturally fascinated by or talented at. When we push our kids to do their best at everything, underneath is generally a feeling that we may not have fulfilled our own potential, or done our best with our own lives.

When our story still looms large, we often miss the clues our children are showing us about how they're wired to thrive. Maybe they're staring at cloud formations and are not that interested in football. Maybe they're not very comfortable socially, but they're fascinated by how things work. Maybe they struggle to remember their belongings, but their imagination is unusually colourful. Maybe they cry easily and don't seem resilient, but they're moved by other people's pain.

All these things may be challenging for them in terms of how the world judges them. But they will thrive, whatever their design, as long as we offer them a strong, non-judgmental connection. This is so much simpler than trying to change our children. We're the ones whose job it is to make sure the criteria of up or down, win or lose, and succeed or fail don't apply at home.

A couple came to see me a few months ago about one of their daughters, who they described as 'negative'. Their daughter was quick to tears and often needed to talk about what had gone wrong during the day rather than what had gone well. They were both sunny, bubbly people and wanted so much for her to be a positive person. As we chatted it became obvious that they were triggered by her different outlook on life and were pushing her to see life in a happier way. We spent some time in the session looking gently at why she triggered them, so they could move towards accepting her just as she was.

Not long after the session I received this email:

"My husband and I came to talk to you about our girl a few weeks ago and you gave us some fantastic feedback: Not calling her 'negative' (in our head), and accepting her for the delightful, 'cup half empty' girl she is. Within a couple of days, she was a different kid! How annoying is it that it was us all along that needed the attitude adjustment and not her?!"

I work with many parents who are still dealing with their own story of not feeling liked by others, or not feeling interesting, or successful. These parents have a set idea in their minds of how their children should be. Thankfully, these are things that can gently and kindly be processed with the ALL technique we learnt in Chapter Three, and through conversations with partners and friends. The goal is to keep these things as far away from our children as we can, and to replace our concern or control with curiosity.

MANNERS

What's usually referred to as 'teaching manners' is a subtle area that produces lots of red brain in parents. Ironically, these lessons are also often taught with very few manners from us. Our need for good manners is often rooted in a need to look good to others, or a fear that our kids will grow up egocentric, rude or selfish; it's often taught rather than modelled. This is not to say that we have to sit back, with a messy house and rude kids, and have faith in the process. As part of the framework of the way we live, we can teach our children to say "please", "thank you" and "sorry", and to share well. What we can't do, however, is sculpt the actual feelings.

Respect, gratitude, remorse and generosity are natural characteristics that grow in children. It's our solid green-brain connection that enables them to grow, but when we role model them, our children learn even faster. Attempts that we make, while in orange or red brain, to get our children to develop these attitudes is like meddling with the plant. It's like polishing the leaves or trying to make the fruit grow faster. Shiny leaves may make us look good, but not even the most gifted gardeners can force the fruit to grow. When we show respect and empathy towards others, gratitude for our lives, remorse for the things we've done that have hurt others, and when we give generously, our kids will naturally grow the same qualities.

I had one mum on my course burst out laughing when we talked about manners. She was remembering all the many red-brained attempts she had made to drag a "sorry" from her increasingly-not-sorry children. She was just the one brave enough to say so but, of course, she was speaking for all of us.

Despite it making sense, none of this has come easily to me. That's why I need the 'my shit' box. I can still be deeply affected by my children's accomplishments, challenges and behaviour. I have to work hard at not needing achievement from them, since I focused on achievement as a child in order to feel good about myself. I also have to work hard at not expecting compliant, polite behaviour, just because that's what was expected of me growing up. I naturally feel comfortable with the order and predictability that comes when they do what they're told, or when they're succeeding, so it's definitely a work in progress. But I am less and less concerned with anything other than the steadiness of my connection with them.

NON-JUDGMENTAL ACCEPTANCE

I've touched on this already, but I want to look further at the idea of acceptance without judgment, as it can be a real stretch for our brains. Non-judgmental acceptance is one of the most precious and unique characteristics a parent can offer their child as part of the connection that allows them to thrive. And it's totally different to how the world in general will treat them, which is why it's so special.

Our children need to know they're already perfectly made in our eyes. We offer them the one relationship in their lives where they can never be essentially improved. They will be graded, compared and critiqued to within an inch of their lives at school and in a thousand ways outside the home, but with us they need to be utterly safe from comparisons. That's the question all our children are asking us in different ways every day: "Am I already ok?" Your answer, in a thousand different ways, needs to be "Yes!"

Lots of parents that I work with worry that if they don't challenge their kids to improve, then they won't fulfil their potential. But the great news is that we really don't need to. When we relax and connect, our children's brains will grow naturally as they're designed to. However, if they sense that we think their better self exists somewhere in the future, there's a strong possibility they will never get there.

If you're struggling with this as an idea, take a moment to think back to your own childhood. Hopefully all of you can connect to someone, even if it wasn't a parent, who thought you were fine just as you were. Maybe it was a grandparent, a teacher, or a friend's parent? If you've never experienced that, just try and imagine it.

What you'll notice is that, although it is a feeling that leads to relaxation, it doesn't lead to lethargy, laziness or selfishness. Feeling total acceptance causes us to rest at the core of our being, but it also energises us in the most natural way. As humans, we are intrinsically wired for work, rest and play. We're wired for creativity and for productivity. We don't need to be afraid of connecting unconditionally with our kids without comparing them or trying to improve them. It's like offering them the perfect combination of healthy soil, sun and rain; they can't help but grow.

One of my dearest friends has five children like I do. They're all grown up now, and I have always loved the way she parented them. I met her when her children were very young; I had no children, and I spent a lot of time with her. For all those years, despite being ordinary kids with plenty of attitude, I never heard her criticise them or talk about them negatively. What was also unusual was that I didn't hear her talk much about their achievements either, although they all did (and are still doing) really well at different things. I didn't fully appreciate it at the time, but I realise now she approached her kids as if they were already enough just as they were, and the relationship she had with them was one of enjoyment more than anything else.

All of her children have now left home and are living their own lives, but they are still deeply connected to their parents and to one another. Now that I know how connection-based parenting works, this makes perfect sense.

THE HEART

We've talked about how we create the safest foundation for our children that we can by offering a strong green structure. That's the box – the connector, if you like. Now we explore the heart, which is our direct connection with our children. The heart is spacious, playful, patient and present. It's full of curiosity and as unconditional as we can make it.

The underlying question here is, *what plant did I get?* along with, *what does my connection with this one look like so that they can thrive?* When we're genuinely connected, we can fully enjoy our children's existence and the interaction between us. This connection looks different for all of us, and there is as much diversity as there are different combinations of parent and child.

The heart connection doesn't need to be about treats, special dates, holidays or even creative activities. It's mundane, everyday green-brain time. It's things like hanging the washing, cuddling, listening, mucking about, and even being on screens together. We're just paying kind attention to our kids and enjoying them in the midst of ordinary life, which is great news for our budgets and our stress levels.

Put another way, the sentiment that drives this connection is: *My kids are wired to thrive and I'm curious to know what that looks like for them. I'm interested in how they feel, what they notice and what they're drawn to.* It may not seem all that special, but its effect is profound. It involves being mindful instead of mindless, so we don't get to the end of their childhood and wonder where it went.

Endless columns and pages are filled with advice about how to do this connection. It baffles me how complicated we've made something so simple. How many arts and crafts we think we need, elaborate treasure hunts and recipes, dress-ups and toys, bikes and boards, activities and day trips. Our children don't need any of these things to thrive. In my experience, if our parenting comes with this level of pressure, lots of unhelpful things happen. For starters, we use up a lot of our time earning money to fund these activities, or plenty of energy thinking up what we should be doing so our children have the best lives possible. We compare our parenting with others, and accessorise and decorate our connection instead of just having it. We often then find fault in the simple enjoyment of time together.

When I look back on the early years with my kids, I remember that apprehensive feeling I had that I should be creating endless memories with my children involving craft projects, successful baking, or energetic bike rides. In reality, we were muddling along just fine at home, and I suspect the greatest pressure came from the failed expectations I was carrying of myself. I parented in orange as a result, with a self-critical busy brain and very little presence, and it didn't take much to trigger me into red. I thought my kids were tricky, or I had too many; but I can see now if I had known connection was all I needed to 'achieve', it would have been quite different. Our home would still have been messy – as it is wherever relationships are being developed – but also less intense and so much more fun.

Don't misunderstand me here. Despite having learnt about the simplicity of connection, some of my best memories of our family life are still special times like floating around on boogie boards in the ocean together. But underlying those picture-perfect moments are connections forged in the snot and tears and mundane ordinariness of life at home, where we're attempting to grow our unconditional green-brain connection all the time.

A WORD ABOUT PRAISE

Sometimes we get our best connection with our children when they've done something amazing or achieved well. In these moments, our children sense intense joy and pleasure from us, and they love it. However, it's important and helpful to also pay attention to whether we've lost touch with that feeling of joy when they're wandering around the house in their pyjamas or sitting beside us in the car. They can begin to get unhealthy messages if the special feelings between us are kept for only the successful or obedient days.

It's a balance, of course: we want to be able to celebrate with them when they do well, or let them know it is great when they listen. One way to do that is just to make sure they know regularly, on an ordinary day, that you're so glad they're around. Mine look at me weirdly and mutter, "Yeah mum, I know", but I do it anyway. I also often add at any moment of achievement, "You know it makes no difference at all to how much we love you, don't you?" And I repeat the same phrase when they've 'failed' or made a choice that wasn't so great: "You know it makes no difference at all to how much we love you, don't you?" It's just a simple way of making sure that they stay grounded in their own essential value.

Although connection is, in many ways, much more intuitive than it is learnt, there are a few ideas that I've come across that have been helpful for me in deepening this heart-based connection.

NON OUTCOME-BASED PLAY

Play is crucial for a child's healthy brain development, but it's a specific type of play called non outcome-based play – or free play – that has the most impact on how their brain grows. Once there's an outcome or goal to pursue, our children's brains don't experience the activity as play in the same way. Competitive sport isn't play. Music practice isn't play. Screen entertainment isn't play. Board games, especially for younger kids, are not play. Who-can-jump-the-highest-on-the-trampoline is not play. Baking, if the results need to be edible, is also not play.

Our children's brains need play that is experiential, exploratory and open-ended. It has no umpires, no rulebook, no winners and losers, no hoped-for outcome, and ideally few – if any – suggestions from us. A child's brain develops when the energy comes from inside them to make decisions, to construct and create. Bored kids, who are safe and well connected, will find the most innovative ways to play with each other or with items in the house or the garden, or at the park or the beach. Our responsibility is to stop entertaining them to death or feeling like we've failed if they're bored.

I love the fact that deep connection can be about healthy distance as much as it is about closeness. Free play doesn't really involve us as parents, other than to carve out the time and space to make it happen, to keep an eye out for safety, and to ride out the whines of boredom while holding back from intervening. Free play grows a child's prefrontal cortex – their executive brain, responsible for making plans and solving problems – which helps in turn regulate emotion and develop learning and creativity.

This is one area of parenting that I did quite well, entirely by accident. Because we had five kids close together, I spent a lot of time at home with them when they were little. The logistics of getting out were tricky. I would play with them up to a point, but I was also busy with nappies and feeding everyone, and all the usual jobs that come with maintaining a home. I also grew up without TV for most of my childhood, so I have a low tolerance for screens. I let them get bored often and let them work out what to do.

They often got frustrated with each other, and then they got creative. They fought with each other and they worked it out. It was never a plan of mine to give my children non-outcome-based play; I'd never even heard of it. Now that I have, I've continued the process. They still struggle when we have no plans - there's no sugar, no screens and no playdates, but they also know this is a regular part of our lives.

For older kids, non-outcome-based play looks more like non outcome-based interactions with us. It's when they can hang out safely and be listened to without judgment or advice. They may not play anymore, in the traditional sense; their lives may be filled with outcome-based activities, with much of their downtime absorbed by screens. But the healthy development of their prefrontal cortex and growth of their self-confidence and resilience is still based around being allowed to be playful, and to be curious about their own thoughts and feelings and to think through their own decisions – either on their own, or with us as part of the process.

When our older kids do invite us to be involved, it makes a huge difference if we can do so mindfully, which means offering them genuine attention and the three mindful attitudes of curiosity, kindness and non-judgmentalism. The stakes are higher with teenagers, so it can be much harder as parents to offer this, but we need to take the risk of trusting them. Doing so will help them get through these difficult years as healthily as possible. When we don't make a conscious choice to engage with them in non-outcome-based interactions, or have at least some ongoing playfulness together, our interactions often deteriorate into instructions, advice or criticism and they soon stop coming to us for connection. If you're genuine and you have no agenda, that's hard for any teen to resist.

DIRECT OR INDIRECT CONNECTION

Another idea that can help foster good connection is that our children really benefit from knowing whether the connection we're offering, in any given moment, is direct or indirect. When we offer them time and attention, that's direct connection. When we're going about our business while they get on with their lives, that's indirect connection. Both are equally healthy, provided we're in green brain.

If our children want our attention, we have to decide whether or not we're there and present. If we decide we are, this means shutting our laptop and giving them eye contact. It means putting our phone facedown, or laying aside the garden spade or chopping knife, and giving them our full attention. It means getting down on the mat, or joining them on the trampoline or their bedroom; it's asking what they want to play, what they want help with, or what they want to talk about. Then we get stuck in.

If we can't give them our full attention, we can still have a healthy connection as long as we acknowledge it and stay green. It's not our children's fault that they want us when we can't be with them. And it's often completely unavoidable that we haven't got the time right now. Being clear about that means a child knows that our lack of physical proximity – or lack of involvement in their dilemma or play, or less-than-focused attention – has nothing to do with how solid our connection is. And that's mostly about the colour of our brain and our tone.

When we're not available, green-brained connection sounds like, "I'm making dinner so I can't come right now, but you can come and sit up at the bench if you want to hang out." Or "I'd love to see how many kicks you can do, but I'm writing the shopping list. I may be a while." Or "I want to hear about your day but we've got to whizz out and pick up (you fill in your blank here). You can tell me all about it in the car". In the following chapter we'll look at how to respond if our children start to complain when we're too busy for direct connection, but often I find they don't seem to be fazed at all if our first response is present and kind, despite being definite. Especially when we don't sound frustrated that they even asked for us in the first place.

I meet many parents who think mindful parenting means having a constant, beautiful, engaged connection with our children all the time. It really isn't like that. That's neither practical nor realistic. In terms of actual interaction and physicality, mindful parenting has as much distance as it does closeness. The difference is that the space between us stays green, so our children don't feel the disconnection that our frustrated red or distracted orange brain causes.

COLLECTING: WHEN OUR KIDS HAVE BEEN APART FROM US

Psychologist Dr Gordon Neufeld outlines the idea of 'collecting', [4] which describes how we can reactivate the relationship with our kids, especially when we've been apart. Key times for collecting are often after school or kindy, when they've been at someone else's house, or even when they wake up.

Picking up my kids after school used to be a nightmare for me. I wondered if I was the only parent who looked forward to seeing their children after a day apart, only to discover they had kept all their best behaviour for their teacher and their friends. I would often see them across the playground, where they seemed completely fine then, as we got closer and they saw me, they would start to whine or cry, or start being extremely rude and demanding. In turn I would reprimand, cajole, attempt to cuddle or, if things were really bad, join in the wailing myself. When I discovered the idea of collecting, their behaviour began to make sense.

As we now understand, our children's brains are wired to develop in a safe and solid relationship with us. When our children are apart from us, their brains work hard to process everything in their day and try to remain feeling ok. Remember how I said their emotion balloon was in pretty much perfect balance? Because of this, they're likely to feel some happiness, sadness, anger and fear pretty much every day. However, a lot of those emotions stay tucked away inside them. School and day-care are generally not environments where they can let them out. When they see us again, their guard comes down, and it all tumbles out.

Being the recipient of all of the negative emotions is actually a privilege, although it really doesn't feel like it at the time. We are our children's safe person and they know it. If they could say, "Mum, I've got a few unprocessed emotions here and I just need to let them out," we'd possibly be fine. But it's totally subconscious, and even they have no idea what's going on or why they're feeling the way that they are. They really do think it's because we forgot to bring any snacks with us or said no to a last minute playdate. Sometimes our children do give us a download of how tough their day was, but even then, asking questions like "What happened?" isn't very helpful. This is a time for listening and empathy, not for fixing and solving.

So how do we do this collecting? For me, it involves eye contact, a smile, and otherwise very few words: "That sounds so tough hun", "You were really brave", "It sucks I forgot to bring food", "Of course you'd love your friend to come home and play". Listen, offer no solutions, and don't ask what did go well today. Instead, just give them a cuddle (if you're allowed), and try to give each child a turn if they need it. Our children will then begin to find their fundamental connection with us again – like finding true north on their slightly wobbly compass after a long day. This process generally doesn't take long if we stay in green brain. Often the good news and positive emotions will follow quickly, after the challenging ones have been allowed an expression.

When our children have been at someone else's house, they often find the transition back home tricky. They're adjusting from being with a friend, new toys and treat food. In this instance, collecting just means being glad to see them, and being patient as they adapt back into life with their siblings, familiar toys and less-interesting food. It means not threatening them with consequences if they're really challenging for a while. We protect the space so that they're not hurting anyone. Other than that, the idea that we missed them is all that really matters. They don't need to have missed us or even want to be home; they'll settle back in soon.

Some children feel disconnected when they wake up, while others don't. Again, it tends to be based around personality rather than the depth of their connection with us, and the same process works well with many of these kids. The idea of collecting worked a treat in the morning for a few years, with one of my children who struggled to get up most days. Before learning about collecting, I used to go into her room, heart in my mouth, and with my sweetest 'time to get up' voice, hope she'd roll out of bed. It rarely worked. I'd drag her out of bed wanting to yell, "The day hasn't even started and you're already grumpy! What are you going to be like by bedtime?"

Collecting changed our mornings with her. I learnt to slow down just a little. I dropped the list of what needed to be done before we left the house, and took a moment to stroke her back while she was in bed. I'd try to make eye contact, say "Hey gorgeous", and then offer her a piggyback as I was starting to leave her room. She still struggled, but mostly the piggyback was too tempting. That said, I often still had a cling-on round my waist while I got the breakfast ready. I could see when her connection tank was full, because she moved off by herself. What I found interesting was that she turned out to be the one who was most likely to get herself completely ready, with no reminders from me, once her tank was full.

I've worked with lots of parents now with similar children. These children are often described as sensitive, but I think they just drain their connection a bit quicker and need collecting more often. This is especially true when life is busy or there are a lot of people in your home. It can be worth remembering that the times when it feels the hardest for us to slow down and offer this to one of our children is actually the time when we really need to.

What I've also noticed is that the kids who need this are often the ones who are much more easily satisfied with simple things. When they're feeling well-connected, they're also more aware of how others are feeling. They often don't have a long list for Santa. These children want one-on-one time with us, they want us to really listen to what they have to say, and they want to know they're significant.

WHEN OUR CHILDREN STRUGGLE WITH SEPARATION

It's also important to point out that if your child struggles to be away from you, it's not always about connection. Some children just enjoy our company more than that of friends. They may prefer being at home, or perhaps they feel less relaxed around other people. In this case, the discomfort when they're away from us is less about disconnection than about preference.

For children like this, helping them through the natural rhythms of being in and out of the house, being with us and being away from us, is simply about making sure we work to understand them, and that we don't push separation in order to help them get over it.

Tune in and you may well come up with some strategies that work for your individual and unique children. As you will see in the next chapter, when we look at how we can support our children through their emotions, our children are great problem-solvers too. They'll often come up with incredibly creative ideas, and they know what techniques will be the most effective for them too. In the meantime, there are some practices that can help with tricky separations.

TOGETHERNESS APART: HELPING OUR CHILDREN FEEL CLOSE

Some form of separation from our children is inevitable. 'Togetherness apart' is my way of describing the internal feeling of connection that we want our children to feel, even when they're not with us. This occurs when the space between us feels green and certain to them. Again, there are no brownie points for whether this comes easily to your child or not; some children are simply wired to be more aware of disconnection than others.

If you do have a child who is strongly aware of disconnection when they're apart from you, there are lots of creative ways you can help them feel they're still connected to you even when you're not physically present. It can be fun to involve your children in coming up with things that are personal to your family.

- Same undies: Get your child to choose both your undies and theirs in the morning. They'll often choose a similar colour. Every time they go to the toilet their brain thinks, Ooh, same undies as Dad. It's a connection!
- Same lunch: If you're going out to work, make yourself a lunch at the same time as they (or you) make theirs. You might include some of the same food, or let them choose something to put in your lunch. When they sit down to have their lunch, they're reminded of their connection with you.
- Same time: Ask them what they're doing that day and tell them what you'll be doing at that time: "I'll be having my coffee exactly the same time as you're having your morning tea". If they've been to your workplace remind them where you'll be, or if you will be at home with your other children, they can easily imagine the place in the house where you drink your coffee. It doesn't matter at all if you don't end up doing the same thing at the same time, what matters is they feel a connection.

On one of my recent parenting courses, a mum raised her hand and excitedly told us all, "I've been doing togetherness apart without realising it". She explained that she had recently started to draw a heart on her daughter's hand, and one on her own hand every day. Her daughter had been struggling to go to day-care, and this seemed to calm her. She hadn't understood why it was helping, but now she realised that every time her daughter looked at her hand, she thought about her mum and felt connected. My favourite part of this story is that a young dad on the course decided he needed to try this for himself. He has since been getting his boy to draw a heart on his hand to remind him all day of the connection. His boy loves it, by the way; it's not a needy parent move, just some fun for both of them.

Togetherness apart is, yet again, not a magic wand. No parenting tricks are. It's a relationship we're dealing with, after all. Yet even addressing our children's separation anxiety, as it's so often called, with creativity can help us stay out of red-brain frustration when they're struggling to leave the house or let us go at the school gate.

TOGETHERNESS APART AT BEDTIME

Just as waking up can be a difficult transition for some kids, bedtime can also be a tricky time. It can feel like hours of disconnection are about to happen, and their bedroom may seem a million miles away from the lounge. It's an exhausting time of day to get resistance from our children, and it can be hard to stay green when they just won't settle.

It ultimately doesn't matter too much if our child's resistance is boundary-pushing or an expression of the looming sense of disconnection they're about to face; either way, connection is still the best place to start. Connection sometimes solves the problem on its own. If not, we need connection to set healthy boundaries anyway.

These are just some of the bedtime ideas I've come across. If you're keen to explore the possibility of closing the disconnection gap, you're likely to come up with other ones that work for your own home.

- Let your child know your routine for the evening: "While you're going to sleep, I'll be... doing the dishes, pouring a glass of wine, sitting on the sofa reading my book..." Probably avoid "skyping Granny" if they love Granny, or "eating chocolate".

- Let them choose a toy from their bed to give you to look after, or give them something of yours to have in bed with them. Make sure their toy takes pride of place beside you wherever you are in case they come and check!
- Keep the door open so they can hear you. Most kids don't need quiet to fall asleep and home sounds can be really comforting to many. If you need to discuss things that are private, wait until they're asleep.
- Ask your child what they think would help them to settle. Children love being asked what they think, as long as bedtime itself isn't up for debate.

A mindfulness practice that signals the end of the day can also be a helpful transition into a deeper connection that replaces physical closeness.

BEDTIME MINDFULNESS WITH KIDS

Early on in my journey with mindfulness, I remember trying to teach some techniques to my children. I'd try to get them to lie down and notice their breathing and parts of their body. There was a lot of giggling and fidgeting. This eventually led to outright rebellion. Let's just say my reaction wasn't my best example of green brain.

Then, my son, at the age of 12, decided to design his own mindful practice, which I still use to this day, as it's the only one my children love. It's called 'the cloud' and it's a full body scan of your child from toe to head. I simply describe how each part of them can settle deeply into the big soft cloud. No part is too heavy that it can't completely relax, and I remind them that each part of their body has done its job for the day. The wording is up to you, but mine sounds like this:

THE CLOUD

"These strong feet have been walking and running all day and now they can relax. Their job is done, and they can sink into the cloud. These legs..." (And so on, moving up the body and using your knowledge of your child's day). You might try something like, "This tummy has eaten all the food it needs for today. This clever heart will keep going all night even when you're asleep. Your busy hands have written so much and drawn so many pictures..." (You can of course adapt this for sports, crafts, or whatever their activities are.) "And now their job is done for today. These eyes have seen/these ears have heard... This mouth has said so many words and now it has done its job. This head has had so many amazing thoughts. It had some worries too, but now it can stop and rest; even it's not too heavy for the cloud."

When I'm finished, I usually pause and stay present briefly and then I leave them to sleep.

These ideas work particularly well if connection is the issue. However, often a child is just annoyed about bedtime – in which case, you'll find help in the next chapter on conflict and setting boundaries. A good way to find out is to offer as much connection as you can, and see what happens.

RECONNECTION: WHEN WE NEED TO RECOVER A BROKEN CONNECTION

Whatever we do, we will all disconnect from our kids regularly, and then our job is to reconnect as quickly as we can. While our children are disconnected from us, their brain struggles to thrive well, as they're generally in red fight-or-flight mode. We need to help them to get back to green brain as soon as we can, back to a healthy, growing, developing brain.

When my children drive me crazy – which still happens regularly – it often takes me time to process my own emotions and return to green. Then it's up to me to initiate the reconnection. This isn't to say they haven't done something tricky or challenging, but it's still my job to role model how to move towards someone after conflict. It's like being an active gardener.

We also can't force the reconnection – our children may take their time to come around. We can only make sure they know we're completely available.

Reconnection looks largely like an apology, but the key element is that it has no learning lesson in it. Try it and you'll discover just how hard this is. I used to think I was good at apologising to my kids, until I realised all my apologies sounded like this:

"I'm sorry I got cross with you, but if you'd listened the first time..."
"I'm sorry I shouted, but that school jumper was expensive..."
"I'm sorry I was late to pick you up, but the traffic was bad..."

Each apology had a learning lesson or justification in it.

If your partner says to you, "I'm sorry I didn't get the milk, but you should have reminded me", there's no actual apology in there at all. They're just being annoying. They've used the magic word "Sorry", but the subtle message underneath is that they're not really sorry because there were mitigating circumstances for their behaviour. Or worse, the blame got shifted during the apology.

I'm slowly learning to apologise for my part in my moments of disconnection with my children, while adding nothing. It's been one of the hardest parts of mindful parenting for me. What helps me is knowing that my goal is getting back to connection and not being right or trying to teach them a lesson. I often end up swallowing air at the end to stop myself adding the "...but...". Now I've come up with a few phrases or ideas that help me. These include:

"I'm sorry I got cross with you. There were so many better ways I could have handled that."
"I'm so sorry I shouted at you, we all lose things from time to time."
"I'm sorry I was late, you must have been so worried."

I'm already noticing the trickle-down or role-model effect.

One of my girls lost her football socks the other day. She started yelling at me to find them for her, and blaming me for not having done the washing. I made a few empathetic noises, carried on with my jobs and left her to it. Then I heard a brief and slightly embarrassed "Found them!" from upstairs. A few minutes later, I felt her arms around me from behind, and she said a quick "Sorry, Mum," and off she went.

I didn't ask for an apology. She offered it and meant it, and I suspect that's because she's finally started to hear genuine apologies from me. As she disappeared, I heard myself say "It's ok hun. Not being able to find things is so frustrating." Mindful parenting is changing me, as that's definitely not what would have come out of my mouth before!

As I draw to the end of this chapter, I think it's really important for me to mention that I have only been able to use these connection-fostering strategies once I've first used the Acknowledge, Link, Let Go process on myself. When our children struggle to separate or emerge grumpy from sleep, we have to process how these things make us feel before we can engage in a connection-based approach. It can take a few seconds to do, but when I offer myself empathy for my feelings, it's not nearly so difficult to feel some empathy towards my kids and to get back to connection again.

Mindful connection is at the heart of great parenting. It makes our job of offering our children what they need so much simpler. The house they live in, the school they go to and the activities they take part in have very little to do with their future success. True success is measured by deep, life-sustaining qualities, such as resilience, energy, creativity, vulnerability, curiosity and confidence. Those things come from at least one solid, as-unconditional-as-possible, connected relationship at home.

Recently I received an email from a mum describing something she and her husband do regularly around bedtime with their seven- and five-year-olds. They call it the 'connection tent', and it's a gorgeous example of choosing connection.

Each evening they cuddle down in bed, one parent with each child, place a pillow over their heads and create a quiet and cosy space. The children share a room, so the pillow creates privacy and special one-to-one time with no distractions. They snuggle face-to-face, look in each other's eyes and chat, or just lie there together for a few minutes. "It has a sense of fun and feels like camping", is how the mum described it.

When she asked her seven-year-old son what he liked about the connection tent he said, "For me it would be that I love just being face to face with Mum & Dad, because I get distracted when the pillow is not on me. I'd be looking around and not focusing on Mum or Dad; I'd be thinking about my LEGO because that's what I can see."

Their five-year-old girl described her experience like this: "I love talking about what I've done in my day. It's better to have the tent because I don't look at my toys. I love to put down the pillow and slide down under the covers and pull the blankey over. It's so much fun."

As I've already said, there are as many examples of healthy connection as there are combinations of parent and child. Our children love green-brain connection, whatever form it takes.

BEFORE WE MOVE ON: MY OWN CONNECTION STORY

I was hidden away in my bedroom one Wednesday evening, doing a final run-through of my notes for the Mindful Parenting session I was about to facilitate, when one of my daughters launched herself onto my bed in tears. The session I was preparing happened to be the one about connection and the words "Sorry hun; I'm a bit busy right now prepping my connection talk" almost spilled out of my mouth. Fortunately I saw the irony, stopped myself, put my notes down and gave her my full attention.

She's the type of kid who usually prefers to work through her emotions on her own but, in this instance, she poured out her feelings about the day, the intricacies and difficulties of her relationships at school, and the friendships that she was struggling with. I listened to her and felt the weight of how hard teenage friendships can be. I tried not to give her advice but made sure she knew it mattered to me.

In mid-conversation, she suddenly sat bolt upright and said, "Mum, can you promise me you're never going to leave me?" She's old enough to understand about mortality, so I said, "I'm not going anywhere. I'll always be here for you." She simply replied, "I thought so, I just needed to check", and she got up, wandered out and that was it. She never talked about it again. She seemed to have got all that she needed.

She was asking the question at the very heart of this chapter: Are you, and will you always be, here for me? It's the deep connection question. And when it's answered with a Yes from us, in whatever form that takes, our children don't need much else from us in order for them to live their own lives well. That connection releases all their own amazing brain resources, which in the end enables them to make much more sense of their own lives than we ever could.

INSIGHT QUESTIONS – CONNECTION

Think of one or two things you would like to put in your 'my shit' box. These are not ideal for writing down, but just make a conscious decision to name them for yourself, and commit to trying to keep them safely away from your children.

Write down three areas of direct mindful connection that you want to add to, or increase, in your relationship with your children individually – or in your parenting journey as a whole.

It could be exploring any of the specific strategies in this chapter, like togetherness apart or collecting. It could be more focused and curious attention. It could simply be anything that you love to do with your kids, or that they love to do with you.

1.

2.

3.

This chapter has lots of ideas in it, so just choose three for now. Don't over-complicate your life by trying to do more, even if more ideas appeal to you. You can always try some of those later. Learning and internalising new things takes work, so keep it simple for now.

5. Resolving conflict without losing your sh*t

Raise your words,
not your voice.
It is rain that
grows flowers,
not thunder.

~ Rumi

Some of you will have picked up this book for this chapter alone. It makes perfect sense if you have, because we all want to know how to manage conflict better with our kids. And most of us want to know if there's a secret formula out there that would make our homes calmer and more peaceful.

If you've skipped through to here though, I would urge you to circle back. This chapter really does stand on the shoulders of the previous ones. The tools and strategies here work infinitely better if we work with them, as much as possible, from a green-brain state. If you haven't yet begun a regular mindfulness practice, haven't begun to process your emotions, or if you're finding an unconditional connection with your children hard to offer, it's likely you'll find the ideas in this chapter challenging.

Being able to get into and stay in our green-brain state lies at the heart of dealing with conflict in a way that helps our children to develop – and more so than just doing what we say. For me, regular green brain means conflict is now far less triggering, and often much less repetitive. Hopefully you'll be motivated to go back and learn the practices that underlie this and that can help you with the parts of this chapter that you like the idea of, but that feel elusive.

The key difference with mindful parenting is that connection remains the primary focus, even in situations of conflict. Traditionally, parenting advice switches to behaviour management when the going gets tough. I'm convinced that the reason so much has been written from a behavioural point of view, and the reason that so many attempted variations exist, is because it doesn't work very well. Behaviour management approaches really don't line up with how a child's brain develops and grows best.

Just as I once did, many parents try different versions of getting their children to modify their difficult behaviours. It's an unhelpful starting point. Trying to modify a child's behaviour changes the colour of our brain to orange at the very least, or more often to red, before we even begin.

The quality of connection that a child has with the adult or adults in their life is the most significant ingredient in the development of sustained behavioural change. It makes sense then that parenting focused on behaviour, rather than relationship, is ultimately self-defeating.

So how do we stay in green brain while managing the challenging situations we face every day as parents?

THE HEART AND THE BOX IN ACTION

Let's go back to the heart and the box idea. In Chapter Four, I used this concept to explain how the connector (the box, which also happens to be us as people) and the mindful connection (or the heart – the relationship we offer our children) work together to offer our kids the best environment to grow up in. We build on this same idea under pressure, and push further into what it means to be the strong solid box whilst still offering the soft connection of the heart.

Here, the box becomes the boundaries we put in place around our children's behaviour. The heart becomes the empathy we offer them for their tricky emotions.

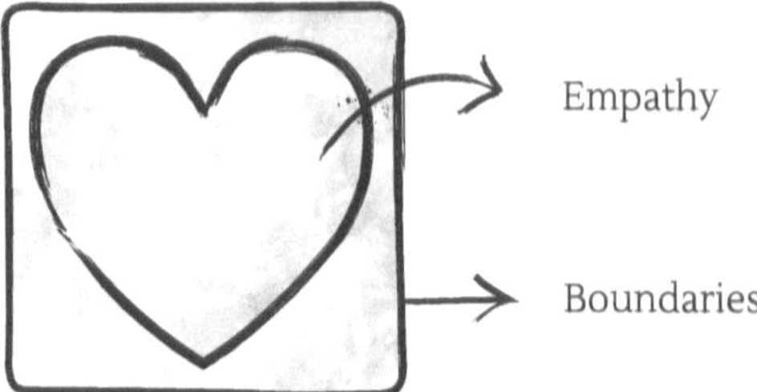

In the heat of a difficult scenario with our children, it can be really hard to tell the difference between an emotion and a behaviour. We need to be able to use both empathy and boundaries at the same time – and learn to dance between the two. However, offering effective empathy and implementing firm boundaries are quite different techniques, so we have to learn them separately before we can integrate them.

MINDFUL EMPATHY FOR EMOTIONS

Empathy is the most effective skill to learn first, because so many conflict situations dissolve once empathy is involved. Sometimes we don't need to set any boundaries after all. Empathy is also a skill we need when our children are struggling emotionally, even if there are no difficult behaviours involved. Although it's the first half of conflict management, it also stands on its own as a skill for any emotional situations with our children.

In Chapter Three, we learnt about our own emotions. So, as we dive into what it means to offer empathy to our children for their emotions, it's helpful to remind ourselves how emotions work.

As we considered earlier, we have four categories of emotions, and our children have the same: anger, fear, sadness and happiness. Children also have the same three ways of dealing with them as we do: they get stuck, they suppress, or they process. The main difference between our children's emotions and our own is that because their brains are dynamic and growing so rapidly, they experience emotions with more suddenness and intensity. They can switch from anger to happiness and back again in seconds. This is a good thing in many ways; however it can be exhausting to respond to, and confusing to handle.

Depending on their age or their life experience, our children may not necessarily have gone through much yet – but just as all of our emotions make perfect sense, either given the current situation or given what we've gone through, so do theirs.

It can be difficult to get our heads around this idea, as so many of their emotions can seem ridiculous, absurd or intentionally dramatic with our adult lens on life. But how much sense their feelings make to us is virtually irrelevant. Empathy is believing someone else's feelings make sense in their lives, even when they don't in ours.

For me, discovering that emotions are always valid - and that includes my children's - has been a complete game-changer. The judgment I used to feel when they over-reacted (or so I thought), completely disabled me from helping the situation move forward. Even if I didn't come out with the words, my inner *Oh for goodness sake* or *Seriously?* generally escalated many emotional situations. My kids could feel my disbelief that they were reacting so strongly to what I saw as the minor challenges of their lives. When I began to recognise that attempting to reduce anyone else's feelings is a pretty reliable way of fuelling the situation further, it was the beginning of an exploration of new approaches to emotion for me.

TRY IT OUT ON YOURSELF...

Imagine you've been at home with the kids all day and it hasn't gone well. There's been some shouting, some crying – yours as well as theirs. Your partner comes home, or your mum drops by, and asks how your day was. You offload all the details, how terrible your children were, what you did in response and how you feel now. Shut your eyes and imagine this scenario. For some of you, it might not be much of a stretch. Try to truly feel the frustration of what you've just communicated.

Now imagine if your partner or your mum responds with:

"It can't have been that bad. Maybe you just need to calm down a bit".

Feel the impact of this answer in your body. See if it's calming you down. Try the same scenario again, except this time your partner or mum responds with:

"Well, maybe if you'd taken them out to the park it wouldn't have been so bad."

Again, shut your eyes and see how you are feeling as you process their response. Is it helping?

Go through the same scenario for a final time. This time, the response you get is:

"Wow, sounds like a tough day. That makes sense; they can be really full on when you have them on your own the whole day." Then they pause. Maybe they follow up with "Would you like a cup of tea?"

Again, see if you can really feel this response as you take it on board.

If the words look a little artificial on the page, imagine it in language or in a tone that feels good to you. What do you notice? For most of us, empathetic words feel like a sort of hug. Our shoulders drop, we finally let go of the breath we didn't even realise we were holding, and we feel understood, like our burden just got a little lighter.

Despite having arguably less intense emotions than our kids, we still feel things pretty strongly. In the same way too, the wrong response has the potential to escalate us towards red. For most of us, the first example response makes us simmer with rage. The second one is patronising, although occasionally I meet someone who finds the suggestion helpful.

The irony is that so many of us regularly tell our children to calm down. Unless your kid has ever said, "That's so helpful Mum, I wish I'd thought of that," I'm guessing it affects them in exactly the same way. Likewise, offering solutions to emotions – "Maybe you could share better next time" – generally doesn't work either. Instead, our children usually meltdown further, argue more furiously or just reject our suggestions – not dissimilar reactions to how we may have felt about the park suggestion.

Solutions are an orange-brain response. We're offering a cognitive solution to an emotional problem. Understandably, the brain resists. When we have an emotion, it triggers the amygdala in the limbic part of our brain. It becomes all about the feeling, as our prefrontal cortex – the part of our brain that thinks in more complex ways – goes offline. We're left with a very simple set of thoughts and reactions to draw from. While solutions designed to fix the problem are tempting, we end up trying to speak to a part of the brain that's not accessible in that moment. There is a much more effective way, and it involves speaking to the active limbic part of the brain. Before we explore that further, with a technique that helps even in the heat of the moment, a final word on empathy.

Dr Seuss says it beautifully: "A person's a person no matter how small." [1] In other words, our children's emotions are just like ours. If a phrase or a reaction would wind you up, your child will feel the same way.

CORE SKILL 4:

Just as ALL (Acknowledge, Link, Let go) from Chapter Three helps us to mindfully process our own emotions, Mirror, Link, Pause (MLP) is the name of the process we use to offer empathy to someone else to help them process their emotions. It's a similar technique and can be offered to anyone, not just children. However, the language is likely to change according to your relationship.

MIRROR, LINK, PAUSE (MLP)

MLP

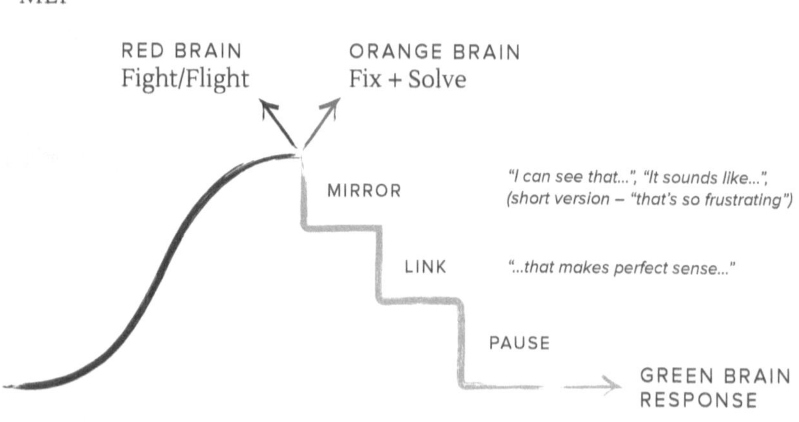

In the previous example of your difficult day at home with the kids, the third response is an example of MLP. As we go through it, hopefully you'll see that it can sound both natural and genuine – despite being a technique that we have to learn.

This example is an adult-to-adult one, in order to get you to feel it, as the recipient. As we go through the process, you'll start to see how it works with children.

MIRROR

The first part is mirror, which in our example sounded like: "Wow, sounds like a tough day."

The mirror uses observation only. Written in black and white, it can look a bit contrived. But, if you use your own language, you'll find a way to make it sound as if you're responding naturally. There are no opinions here ("Well, I think…"), there are no solutions ("Try the park next time…"), no attempts at cheering up ("At least they're all still alive…"), no belittling ("It can't have been that bad…"), and there's no comparative suffering ("You think your day was hard?"). Instead, the mirror stage is simply a reflection back.

When we're mirroring, the easiest way to respond is by mentioning, or even repeating back, what we've just seen or heard. The mirror often uses words like "I can see you're…", or "It sounds like…" It's common though, that you'll adapt quickly as in the bottom two examples, if you or your children don't like the repetition.

> *"I can see you're gutted you lost that football game."*
>
> *"It sounds like you were really scared when your teacher shouted at you."*
>
> *"I can see you really wanted more screen time."*
>
> *"It sucks he broke your train, doesn't it?"*
>
> *"It's so frustrating having to tidy your room."*

The mirror sometimes reflects the emotion and sometimes the event. In the example I took you through, I reflected the event; "Sounds like a tough day". I could also have mirrored the feeling and said, "Sounds like you're feeling exhausted/frustrated/fed up". Try to mirror not just the emotion, but also the intensity you've noticed. You're not attempting to reduce the emotion here, but simply to reflect it well. "You are so cross with me right now", is much more helpful, if it's accurate, than "You look a little annoyed".

LINK

After we've successfully mirrored, next we offer a link, which in our example was: "That makes sense, they can be really full on when you have them on your own the whole day."

Just like the link in ALL, the link here means you're validating that the emotion the other person is feeling makes perfect sense, which takes the empathy to a deeper level. The link part is a bit of a guess when you're working with someone else's emotions – but when you know someone well you will often be spot on, which makes them feel really known.

> *"I can see you're gutted you lost that football game. That makes so much sense as you beat these guys just a few weeks ago."*
>
> *"It sounds like you were really scared when your teacher shouted at you. That makes sense, because you hate being shouted at" or "you've worked so hard at your reading".*
>
> *"I can see you really wanted more screen time. That makes perfect sense, you love that game you were playing."*

With screens, especially, keeping it genuine and not sarcastic can be hard, but screens are somewhat addictive, so we need to get our heads and hearts around that.

> *"It sucks he broke your train. It makes perfect sense you're mad; it was the special one you got for your birthday."*
>
> *"It's so frustrating having to tidy your room. Jobs really aren't much fun, are they?"*

(Try to avoid the learning lesson here).

If communicating with your children like this feels uncomfortable, inject some humour. It doesn't all have to be serious. I often overdramatise, which is probably more about distraction than empathy, but it's enjoyable and often helps:

> *"It's so frustrating having to tidy your room. It looks like your toys got up in the night and had a party!"*
>
> *"Oh my goodness, that sounds like you had the absolute worst day ever!"*
>
> *"I think we need to call an ambulance; you might be dying!"*
>
> *"Nooooooo, not broccoli. It's so unfair you have to eat that!"*

Sometimes my kids say to me, "Mum, it's not that bad!" or just "Muuum", but that's a win in my book. Of course, you have to know your children well. Some are more literal, and you need to keep the humour away, or they may feel you're laughing at them. Work your own children out; it's all part of your connection, and then you can play a bit more with the technique.

Often kids have something going on underneath their display of emotion, which even they may not know about until we offer them empathy. In this case, the link is often a suggestion rather than a fact. I find that sometimes when I gently say, "You're really upset because you wanted something different for afternoon tea," they move from anger to tears, and something blurts out like, "I came bottom in spelling today". The empathy has helped them get to what's really upsetting them. It's a better way to get down the layers of emotion than asking if there's something else going on, as often they have no idea.

I had a recent example, though, where I braved linking to what hadn't yet been said. One of my daughters was in tears and adamant she wasn't going to her dance class that evening. I was feeling tired and took a pause before gathering myself to empathise with her feelings when I remem-bered the following day was athletics day at school. She had done well the year before and I know she feels the expectations of others heavily, and I wondered if there was a link.

I gingerly pulled her onto my knee, and after pulling away initially she rather suspiciously let me hold her. As there were other kids around, I whispered in her ear, "Are you worried about athletics day?"

I felt her body relax a little and between sobs she managed to mumble into my shoulder, "Of...course...I...am!"

I then added, "And you did so well last year it's really hard to know people might expect you to win?"

Again, I felt her body relax even more. She nodded at me. So, I kept going.

"That makes so much sense, hun." She gave me that look as if she was expecting a lesson on winning and losing. I just paused and took a deep breath and said, "It's tough isn't it?" and then just sat there with her. After a minute or two she disentangled herself, carried on with the afternoon and went off to dance that evening without a word.

She still needed some empathy the next day when things didn't go quite according to plan at school, but I noticed how much quicker she recovered from her disappointment because we had already laid a foun-dation of empathy together.

Although we can be endlessly creative with empathy, there are some words that don't work too well. Try and avoid, "I understand how you're feeling," as this makes the situation about you and not them. It's also of-ten more annoying than helpful. None of us can fully understand some-one else, so "It makes perfect sense..." works better. Again, try it out on yourself or get a friend to try it out on you and you'll feel the difference.

"It makes perfect sense" is a beautiful phrase which some children never get enough of and some children get fed up with quickly, so finding ways to say the same thing with different words is really helpful. Often older kids feel more comfortable with a shorter version of the mirror and link. As long as the empathy is as genuine as you can make it, it works just as well.

Some shorter examples might include:

"Gosh, friendships can be hard work."
"Not making it into the team sucks."
"You're pretty gutted we said no to that party, aren't you?"

PAUSE

Once you have mirrored and linked, the final part of the process is to pause. The Pause is crucial, despite often feeling like the hardest thing to do, especially in the early stages of practicing MLP.

In the scenario we were initially looking at, I paused before offering a cup of tea. This gives time for the empathy to land and stops us from moving from green straight into orange. If I had gone straight for the cup of tea option, it would have sounded like a solution; as though I was suggesting that your day was hard, but a cup of tea will fix it.

With a pause, it's clear the conversation can keep going over a cup of tea and the cup of tea itself then just becomes an act of connection and love. With children, as you'll see in the examples that follow, the pause stops us piling in with our ideas. It cuts off the tempting parental "But..." that we're all so familiar with, and the surprising power of the pause is that it opens up space for our children to begin to solve their own problems.

Go back and have a look at any of the mirror and link phrases, either the full-length versions or the shorter ones, and imagine adding nothing at the end other than staying present. It's hard to do. But what often happens is that in the pause, a child may often move on, ask for help, or find their own solution.

In the scenarios above, you may have been thinking, "What's next? What comes after the pause?" It's tempting to overstep our role as gardener and start sculpting away in the belief we know what's best.

If your children are used to you handling emotional situations differently – especially if you usually do a lot of cheering up or solving – they can feel a bit disorientated when you start using MLP. Although you will develop a deeper connection over time, as well as much more resilient children, the transition from being helped to finding their own resources can be hard for some kids at first. It can feel like a withdrawal, rather than a space full of support and empathy.

I spoke to one mum the other day who had just started using the practice. Her 14-year-old was upset and she empathised, linked and then paused. Her daughter waited, looked at her in shock and then yelled, "Why aren't you saying anything, Mum!? Why aren't you HELPING ME?"

There are some phrases I use often to help the pause along, especially if I can see one of my kids is struggling and wanting more from me.

My favourites are:

"You have great ideas, what do you think?"
"Do you need any help to get through it?"

With my twins, I often say "I've never been a twin; I have no idea what it's like to have to share everything... What do you think?" A variation on this could be said to any child: "I've never been a boy..." or "It's a long time since I was 13..."

If their solution is to ask for your advice, that's fine, because asking for help is a skill in itself. If they're still in red brain, flooded with emotion and yelling for your help, it's best to return to the mirroring and linking process. If you can see some air has come out of their balloon – and they're still asking for your help – then you can get involved. With any suggestions, it's still wise to remind your child that they might have much better ones than you do.

Try to avoid sharing your own story as part of the pause, unless your child is really back in green. A few months ago, I had one very irate child struggling with her maths homework. As maths really wasn't my strongest subject at school, I was busy empathising away with ease: "Maths can be so hard, hun. That makes perfect sense you're struggling".

As I continued gently to make sure she felt supported, I could see her melting a little. Her shoulders relaxed, and her body grew less tense. I then interrupted the process with my sunniest "I wasn't great at maths and I've done fine". She tensed up again and dashed upstairs yelling, "That's your life Mum, not mine!" She was completely right. I was hoping it would bounce her through the last fragments of her emotion, and instead it felt to her like I was attempting to fix things, which I was. Without her even really knowing it, her reaction was telling me just to be there while she got through her own emotion, and not try and hurry it along.

The pause really is incredibly powerful. With each emotion that our child processes themselves, their brain grows. They feel the tricky chemicals land, they hear our empathy, they internalise that it's not so bad having an emotion, and they let it out. We need to respect them enough to let them do this, and just watch in amazement as they start to process emotions with much more health than most of us were ever allowed as children. It gives our children a chance at an adult life with full access to all their emotions, which of course includes more joy than many of us have known.

MIRROR, LINK, PAUSE WITH EACH EMOTION

Let's look at some scenarios of using MLP with each of the four emotions.

HAPPINESS

With happiness we tend to do it automatically: "Wow, sounds like an amazing day! (M) You love dancing, you love chocolate and you love Granny, so that sounds perfect (L)". I haven't used the phrase, "It makes perfect sense" here, but I've offered plenty of links as to why the day made them so happy. The pause often isn't necessary with happiness, other than to make sure we're not rushing on to something else and that we're savouring the moment.

SADNESS

"You're so upset hun, because (so-and-so) was really mean to you at school (M). That makes so much sense because you really like playing with him (L)." And then pause (P).

"That looks really sore (M). You were riding fast so that must have hurt a lot (L)." Pause (P).

"It's so rough seeing all those party photos on Instagram (M), when you would have loved to have been invited (L)..." Pause (P).

FEAR

"Oh hun, you sound as if you're really scared about school camp (M). That makes perfect sense, you've never been before (L). " Pause (P).

"You're really scared to walk past that house (M) because that's a big dog and he's barking really loudly (L)." Pause (P).

"It sounds like you're really worried you're not going to do well in your exams (M). That makes so much sense, exams can feel scary (L)". Pause (P).

ANGER

"It's so hard when we have to leave (M). It makes so much sense as you've had loads of fun (L)". Pause (P).

"She took your train agaaaain; that's so frustrating (M). And it's the only one with batteries, no wonder you're upset (L)". Pause (P).

"You're pretty upset because I said no to the party (M). That makes perfect sense, you really wanted to go (L)." Pause (P).

The dog example, listed under the fear section, came from one of the parents on my course. Every day the mum and her little boy had to walk past a house with a big dog, and every day her son was scared. The mum had understandably been trying to calm her son down by telling him the dog was behind a fence, that she was right beside him and that he was quite safe. None of it had worked. After she learnt the MLP technique she tried it out the next morning. She got down to her son's eye level and said, "You're so scared, and that makes perfect sense. He's a big noisy dog and feels so close to you when you walk past". The little boy walked straight past the dog and he was fine from then on.

WHY EXPLANATIONS DON'T WORK

As I mentioned earlier, when we have an emotion, it triggers the amygdala in the limbic part of our brain. Not only do solutions not work very well, but explanations are also wasted when the limbic system is activated.

For example:

"I asked you three times and you said you wanted cake, we bought you cake so you can't now have ice-cream". As far as I know, this has never made a child calm down and see the light.

"It's so hard when you choose something and then see something else that looks yummy" is far more helpful, and sometimes completely resolves the situation without needing to add the boundary of not buying icecream. You're speaking to the activated part of the brain – the feeling part – and it soothes. Emotions don't respond to logic; they respond to empathy.

A few weeks ago, my son slept in late and was mucking around in the kitchen with his sisters before school. As he's older he now has to get to school earlier than they do, and this particular morning he suddenly realised he was going to be late. He ran upstairs to me in a panic, asking me to give him a lift. I said I couldn't, and he yelled at me, "But I'll be late!"

I calmly responded, "Yes, maybe," and muttered something about that being tricky for him. I managed to leave it at that. I was so tempted to add all sorts of explanations – about him sleeping in or playing around, or reminding him that he had a perfectly good bike he could use even though he hates riding to school! – I resisted though, and off he raced.

That evening he breezily walked in the house and said that he'd arrived with 30 seconds to spare and that he'd clearly mistimed the walk! It was a win-win. I managed to prevent the cascade of enlightenment I wanted to offer him, which I know would have exacerbated the problem and taken a lot of energy from me. He came up with his own solution, I imagine by walking pretty fast. He didn't need a lecture, nor to be rescued, and he hasn't slept in late since then.

WHAT IF I FIND IT HARD TO DO?

If MLP is hard for you, it may be because you find it hard to empathise with your own emotions using ALL. It's a common struggle for parents. You can fake it for a while, but at some stage you will need to return to your own ALL until you can experience just how valid your own emotions are. Empathy is designed to overflow from your full tank and green brain, not to be dredged up or feel contrived. However, while you're finding your own empathy for yourself, you can still practice on your children. Just follow the steps.

WHAT IF IT DOESN'T MAKE SENSE?

One of the most common questions I get asked is "What if their emotions don't make any sense?" It's a valid question, but it also has a very simple answer. It doesn't have to make sense to us; we simply have to know and accept that it makes sense to their brain.

Their emotion will always make sense somewhere in the jungle of that day, week or year. And it's not a stretch to imagine the relief that comes from hearing empathy in a response. Rather than telling you they wouldn't feel that way or that it's not logical, it feels great when a friend or partner lets you know that your weird and wonderful emotions make sense. Dig deep into your childhood memories, however foggy they are, and you'll remember feeling strong anger, embarrassment, shame, anxiety and even happiness about the mildest, simplest or strangest of things.

WHAT IF IT MAKES IT WORSE?

MLP works incredibly well in so many situations, either leading your child gently back to green, or at least making sure we get back to green ourselves rather than struggle with two red brains. Having one in green is far more helpful.

With some children, however, MLP sends their emotions into overdrive. It's not always clear why that is, but there are two common reasons I've come across.

The first is that the empathy itself often has an implied boundary in it. You're unlikely to mirror how hard it is to have no more biscuits if you're planning to let them have another one. Likewise, you're not going to empathise with how rough it is to have to go to bed if you're planning to let them stay up longer. Our children's brains sense the implicit boundary. While the empathy is often enough to settle them, sometimes the realisation dawns that the boundary is clear, and that can initially upset them further. If this happens, don't be too fazed. Just keep empathising and the resistance often dissolves.

The second reason seems to be that if a child is used to having their emotions shut down, they may have little or no experience of processing emotions. When this is the case, the invitation and the openness can cause a huge explosion or a meltdown. Your child may feel overwhelmed and lost in all the cortisol in their system, and, chances are, they are unskilled at knowing what to do with it. Don't be put off. Processing our emotions is very natural when it's allowed, so it will be a skill they develop easily when we support it with empathy.

I had an email recently from a mum whose teenage boy was refusing to go to school because he didn't want to face a situation that had happened the day before. The mum mirrored and linked instead of telling him to get a grip, and the boy went a little crazy. He stormed off, smashed a picture frame in his room, and then locked himself in the bathroom, refusing to come out. He shouted through the door that his mum could take away anything he liked, his Xbox, his pocket money and so on. The mum did an incredible job of sticking with the emotion and mirroring it. She didn't move to the breakage or the behaviour. Eventually the boy came out. His mum got him to school and said nothing else.

She emailed me that day quite shaken, as she'd never used MLP before and was, understandably, convinced it had been a terrible idea. However, she did acknowledge she would normally have discouraged her boy's feelings and taken something away from him to get him to go to school. She wondered if her empathy had somehow enabled her son to experience his emotions more thoroughly and he was letting her know the system of consequences was not really helping him. The boy's mum asked me if she should talk about the picture frame, the refusal, and the language her son had used. I wasn't sure, but I had a gut instinct the boy had done a lot of work that morning and maybe just needed a check-in to see how he was feeling now, rather than a telling off.

After school that day the boy came home and apologised. He also asked his mum if he could talk to her about the situation at school, which was something he'd not really asked her to be involved in before.

I imagine at some point the frame will need to be mended, and her son may be involved in that. But he felt, and expressed, a very strong emotion and was held all the way through it. This is so hard to do but does wonders for any connection. When we are at our worst and someone stays close by, without judgment, our heart and our brain grow in confidence, in resilience and in responsibility.

I'm not going to pretend MLP is a magic wand every time, but I can honestly say it's been as close to a magic wand as I can ever imagine having in our house. Of all the techniques I teach, MLP is the one that seems to make the biggest difference and the most rapidly. It's a beautiful form of connection during situations that often cause disconnection.

I have so many examples of this from parents I've worked with, and I've included just a couple of my favourites here.

One morning I had asked my six-year-old son to get ready for school about three times, and he just wasn't making any moves to do so. He had this huge blanket that he was busy draping over the dining room chairs to make a fort (his favourite activity). As I asked him one more time – my voice rising all the while – he started getting quite agitated. He stomped around a bit, swinging his arms and generally getting ready for a confrontation.

I took a moment and then said, "Hey, I can see you're getting quite upset and angry. That makes sense to me because you just love building forts." At this point, my natural reflex would be to go into an explanation that if he didn't start getting ready now, we would be late. But instead I just paused. He stopped and looked at me with an expression of complete surprise; all the anger had gone. I think the wind had been completely taken out of his sails! Then he

*just nodded, shrugged and said, "Yeah," and then proceeded to go
and get himself ready!*

And

*We were in the car when my three-year-old was kicking off about
something. I had just started saying, "I can see you're getting angry..." to him. My six-year-old daughter then chimed in with, "Mummy, you're going to do that thing where you say 'That makes sense,'
aren't you?" I stopped, really surprised, and felt like she had seen
right through me and thought that I was following a script. Then
she went on to say, "I like it when you do that, because it helps me
to feel my emotions." My jaw dropped. I just said, "Oh, that's good."
Even though she knows what I'm doing, she likes it. Amazing!*

MLP isn't a behaviour management technique; it really is a tool to help us express empathy skilfully. When your child falls apart because they got the wrong colour plate, you may have to empathise through gritted teeth or through your giggles, but "You love the green plate and there's only the pink one left (L), that's tough hun (M)", is so much better than, "Oh, for goodness sake – it's just a plate!" or slipping in a "Well if you hadn't thrown it across the room yesterday, you could have the green one!"

As you can see, the MLP technique is endlessly flexible. Once you've grasped the steps, you can play around and make it your own – and try it out on adults, too. If you're in green brain, it will come out well however you do it. It really is the heart going into action for your kids while they're struggling. Our children's patterns of dealing with their emotions are not yet strongly wired into their brain and, although it may sound lofty, using MLP will give them the opportunity to become processors, rather than stuckies or suppressors, and may well change family patterns for gener-ations to come.

Sadness and fear are easier to handle than anger. Once we've empathised there's often not much more we can offer, other than to see if they need support to work out how to move on or what to do next. Anger is the hardest one to stay green and do MLP with, but in many ways angry moments can be the most significant for our children. When they express their anger, and instead of getting an angry or frustrated response back from us they receive empathy, compassion and understanding, their connection with us and their personal brain development get a little growth spurt.

Lots of tricky situations in my house now end with empathy, without needing a boundary. Your child moves past whatever they're struggling with and the situation resolves. Empathy alone doesn't solve everything, however. Sometimes it's not just a feeling that we need to connect with and help our children to process; there's also a behaviour that needs addressing. This is when we need the second part of our response to difficult situations: firm boundaries.

MINDFUL BOUNDARIES FOR BEHAVIOUR

All emotions are ok, but not all behaviours are, so we need to know how to put effective boundaries in place, represented here by the box, as much as we need to know how to empathise effectively. Once we can do both, we can move in and out of the dramas and conflicts of our homes with more ease.

Sometimes we start straight in with boundaries, especially if anything is unsafe or a child is being violent. More often we start with empathy, however we need to learn when to switch to boundaries so that we don't get stuck in endless rounds of MLP when our children need to move on in a different way.

A metaphor that I find helpful for this is that, as parents, we are the pilots of the plane, and our children are the passengers. One wing is empathy and the other boundaries. We dip towards one wing at times and then steady up with the other. If we spend too much time in either empathy or boundaries, the plane gets stuck going round in circles. Ideally, if there are two parents in the house, both parents learn both skills. It's not ideal for kids to see a huge bias in either parent, as it tends to lead to the 'good cop/bad cop' arrangement.

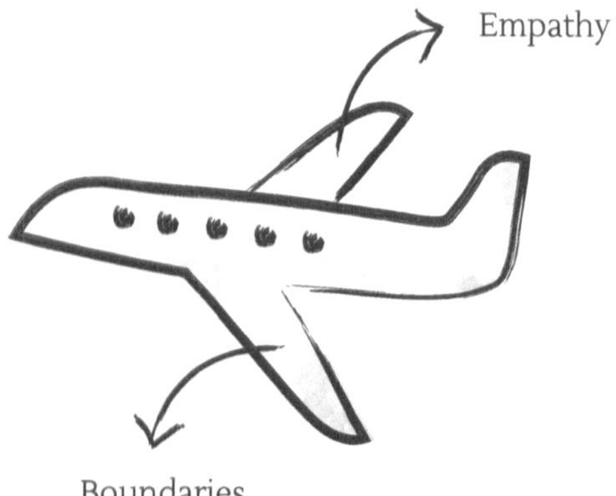

Our boundaries are just as significant a part of our connection as empathy is. It may not seem it at first, but the box can be described as love just as much as the heart is. Boundaries are not the cross part of parenting, the thing we have to resort to when nothing else has worked. Boundaries have a long-term purpose as well as sorting out current conflicts, and children's brains need boundaries to thrive and to feel safe.

In my counselling practice, I see two different types of kids emerge from homes where boundaries are inconsistent, especially if the boundary changes according to the intensity of the child's argument. The first are 'alpha' kids. These are children who are bossy and prescriptive. To continue my plane metaphor, these children have decided the cockpit is empty and they need to step up. This can be extremely messy, because children aren't yet ready to be in charge. Despite outward appearances, the responsibility they feel puts their brains under enormous stress, and they often swing between bossiness and outbursts of rage or tearfulness.

The other type of child that I see emerge from a home in which boundaries are open to too much negotiation is an anxious or nervous child. Their brain gets the message that there's no one reliable in the cockpit, but instead of heading for the cockpit they stay in their seat and get increasingly nervous. These children may find it difficult to try new things, they might get worried by small events, or they can become overly responsible or eager to please.

Holding the role of the pilot and keeping the boundaries of the box our children inhabit clear and firm – even in the onslaught of emotions and resistance – is what our children really need from us.

THE BOUNDARY OF ROUTINE

The first and easiest way to set boundaries is outside the conflict zone. Many of these boundaries are pre-determined and repetitive. This is really just about establishing routines. Having a routine doesn't mean we need to lead dull, structured lives with no spontaneity; it just means there are certain things that generally happen at roughly the same time each day, or each week. Our brains love repetition and, as we've seen, we create deep neural pathways around anything that happens over and over. In these cases, the fight dials down much quicker, even if the routine activity is something that's not much fun.

A perfect example of this is seatbelts and teeth-brushing. Most kids battle with these for a while, but because we don't give in, and we find ways to consistently reinforce them, these battles tend to die down a lot quicker than others. If we apply the same approach to areas like screen-time, bedtime routines and household jobs, our children's brains give up the fight quicker than if everything is open to change.

THE BOUNDARY OF REGULAR RESPONSES

Regular responses play a similar role to routine. These are set responses that we have in areas where conflict is common, so we don't have to re-invent the wheel each time.

These are just some examples I use to help me stay calm and de-escalate situations that used to turn red very fast.

"ASK EACH OTHER TWICE BEFORE YOU INVOLVE A PARENT."

When my kids run in yelling "Muuuuummm, he..." or "Mum, she...", protesting about another child's behaviour, my rule is that before I get involved, they must have asked the other person twice to stop. If not, they have to go back to the scene and ask for the toy back, their favourite jumper, to be allowed to join in, or for a turn on the trampoline.

Often I never see them again, either because they've sorted it, or because on the journey back they've forgotten what the problem was and got distracted. Sometimes I hear, "Give it back, give it back! I've asked twice; they won't, Mu-um!", delivered at breath-taking speed, and I find it hard to keep a straight face. I usually ask them to try again a bit slower and see what happens.

If they do come back, it's given me a bit of time to think. I find it easier to respond in green brain and I start with my mirror, "That sounds tough hun..."

"WHEN YOU'VE ASKED TWICE, THEN INVOLVE A PARENT."

My next regular response is the opposite of the first one, and means that I jump in if things are escalating. We live in a two-storey house, so when I hear things kicking off, I often have to yell this one if they're upstairs. It sounds like this: "What happens now guys?" As they know the system, I usually get a reluctant, "Come and get you?" back.

Although it's not a solution in itself, it's a boundary that provides a break in the proceedings and gives everybody's cortisol levels a chance to calm down a bit. It can also provide an incentive for them to start working out what to do together, rather than walk all the way downstairs to me.

"NOT A WITNESS."

If I wasn't there at the scene of the crime, I won't give an opinion or take sides. I love this one. It means all I can offer is diplomacy when the "Ask each other twice" routine hasn't worked. Almost all children make it sound like nothing was their fault, and they really believe it, so it's just a rabbit hole we go down if we follow them into "She hit me/He swore at me first" territory. I'm not interested in what happened; the truth is rarely accessible. I'm only interested in whether they need my help to move forward, either together or apart.

You'll need to find your own script for this, but helping them to move forward in green brain sounds a bit like, "That sounds tricky (M). It sounds like it's not working for either of you (M). Have you got any ideas? (P)". I often skip the link as that's the piece I don't know in this case. It's also where the "Whose fault is it?" part often emerges. That said, something impartial like, "Taking turns isn't easy" may work here.

Just to clarify, I wouldn't use any of these three responses if you're working with a child who tends to be regularly violent or dominating in some way. These are generally for fair and well-matched battles.

"TRY AGAIN."

This is a huge favourite in our house, at least of mine. When any of the kids say something in a lazy or rude tone, "Try again" does the trick more often than not. I used to spend so much time telling them how rude it was to treat me like the maid – or speak to anyone like that, for that matter – as my red brain was triggered by the disrespect. "Try again" is so simple and needs no explanations about politeness, and they all seem to get it.

I was out with all my kids the other day, and one of them yelled at me to wait, with that demanding tone kids do so well. You know the one:

"Muu-uuummm! Waiiiit!!"

I called back in my sunniest voice. "Try again."

She immediately changed her tone completely and called, "Can you wait, Mum?".

A woman passing by said in amazement, "How did you do that?" I believe there's something about those two words – a simple "Try again" – which are truly non-judgmental and give our children a dignified second chance.

"EMOTIONAL REACTIONS ARE OK, BUT NOT GENERAL RUDENESS."

This is an attempt to find a way to try and distinguish emotion from behaviour. I want my children to have the freedom to process anger around each other and not shut it all down, but I also want them to grow up in a home that feels emotionally safe. So, I have a general rule that if one of them has annoyed another, a reaction makes perfect sense. I use MLP and then see if a boundary is needed, or if they can work it out for themselves, so they get good at conflict resolution.

However, if one of them is just finding another annoying for no real reason, it goes in the behaviour category. I don't spend much time on empathy apart from a "Yes, sharing a house can be hard", but they all know if they're feeling grumpy and unable to treat each other with the bare minimum of respect, that they have to take themselves off to their room or remove themselves from the scene, until they can do so.

After school is a common time for this, especially for older kids who've been with their peer group all day and find coming back to their younger siblings annoying. It makes sense, but assuming the little ones have done nothing other than be their age, a boundary is more effective here than a lot of empathising.

"FREEDOM AND RESPONSIBILITY GO TOGETHER."

This pairing has worked wonders in our home in terms of helping us navigate all the injustices children naturally feel, especially with different ages and stages in the same house. It means that at certain ages each child will get a new freedom (a later bedtime, different movies, an allowance, a phone etc.) and with it comes a responsibility (a regular job of some kind, which could be washing up, cooking a meal a week, setting the table, or sticking to a particular curfew). When these things are tied together, we don't need red brain to enforce the jobs. It's just a factual arrangement, which they all know about.

My middle child is about to turn 13. She will get a later bedtime, the dishwasher to empty along with clearing and wiping the table every mealtime, and a phone (we realise we're possibly a bit late with technology). As you can imagine, she's ambivalent about the arrangement, but she said to me the other day in the car, "I'm growing up, Mum, aren't I?" It was a strangely comforting sound for me. She's aware that freedom and responsibility go together, and that feels like growing up to her.

Children who get more and more freedom and little responsibility to go with it often become hard to parent. When this happens, their brains aren't growing in maturity at the same rate as more of the world is becoming available to them. It can also make life hard for them later, as the two generally go together in adult life.

I regularly work with parents of teens who have reached a stage of life where they have a lot of independence but no regular contribution to the house or family. The only way their parents can get them to do jobs or be reliable in their communication is to nag or to give them some form of red-brain consequence, both of which cause disconnection and achieve very little.

I also work with parents who take the opposite approach. They require more and more responsibility from their kids - good grades, success in their extracurricular activities - but don't offer increasing levels of trust and freedom. These kids tend to have two very different responses. They either rebel and leave the parental relationship behind, or they achieve highly but with anxiety levels to match. The goal is a green-brain relationship always, so I encourage the parents to go back to their teenagers and together create a regular and reliable system as to what responsibilities and freedoms feel appropriate, fair and manageable. Most teenagers respond well to these respectful conversations. Often we think we've already had these chats over and over, but if they took place in orange brain (when we're nagging) or in red brain (which means they sense they're in trouble), it's unlikely they'll have had much effect.

Most kids do understand that there's a connection between some form of regular contribution and trustworthy communication, and being able to come and go with increasing freedom, having their parents' support as they develop their interests, and having simple things like food on the table.

REAL LIFE HAPPENS

Having routines to stick to and responses you can use regularly can be helpful, and they reduce the amount of in-the-moment boundaries you have to set. But the reality is that lots of conflict falls outside of any of these categories and the ready responses may not apply. In this case, we need to be able to introduce and stick to green-brain boundaries in situations we can't plan for. To do this, we need to understand how our children's brains actually respond to boundaries, and how we can set them in a way that helps them get through the pain.

CORE SKILL 5:
MINDFUL BOUNDARY-SETTING

Firstly, there are no perfect solutions here. No parent can get their child to behave how they want all the time, no matter what the approach. Secondly, what boundaries you choose really is up to you; it's how you set your boundaries that's far more important.

BOUNDARIES HELP OUR CHILDREN DEVELOP A MORE RESILIENT BRAIN

In order to set boundaries well, we need to understand that boundaries not only offer our children safety and love, but they are also one of the many things in our children's lives that contribute to their journey toward developing resilience.

The word 'Resilience' describes our ability to bounce back from difficult situations or setbacks in our lives. Whatever age we are, whenever we're faced with challenging events our brain initially responds with a desire to try and change whatever it is that we don't like. We often start with resistance and we try and influence the situation, sometimes with persuasion, persistence, frustration or anger. Only then, if events are truly beyond our control, do we give up the fight, and move towards acceptance. After that, we're able to slowly recover or bounce back, depending on the severity of the situation. If we move through this process, however clumsily, when we struggle – and we do so without getting stuck in bitterness, resentment or blame – we grow in resilience.

We all go through this process many times in our lives. At its most extreme, it's the grief and loss cycle, with its profound resistance and the eventual letting go. It works the same way with less emotionally significant events, such as not getting invited to a party, losing a friendship or a job, failing an exam, coming across unexpected roadworks or changes to our plan for the day, or just not getting our own way.

The more familiar we become with recognising and acknowledging the events and people in our lives that we can't change (while retaining our ability to influence those we can), the more skilled we become at adapting to the natural frustrations, disappointments and heartaches of life and the less we need to be in control. This isn't the same as 'sucking it up'; this is about facing our feelings of vulnerability and finding a way through so that our lives aren't dominated by things we can do very little about. As we go through this process, we develop resilience.

When we set a boundary for our children – usually around something they want to do that they can't, or something we want them to do that they don't want to do – they're faced with the same challenge.

Let's use bedtime as an example. It's an event that happens every day, and it can be infuriating when our children struggle to go to bed, despite its regularity. But every day is a new day for our kids, and bedtime is the end of a chance to keep playing or chatting or watching something fun. It can feel just as hard to accept, no matter how reliably it comes around. They feel frustration and a deep desire to change the situation they don't like - and the resistance begins. It's a very natural human instinct. Our job is to stay steady, stay as green as we can, and support them through the process, without changing the boundary.

In my work with parents I use a simple arc to show how this sequence unfolds. It's adapted from Dr Neufeld's work in which he describes a child moving from 'frustration' through to 'futility' and eventually to 'tears'.[2] I find 'giving up the fight' also describes the idea of 'futility' well. Similarly, 'acceptance' is an alternative to 'tears', as often a child's full emergence on the other side of the cycle will involve some emotional softening, but doesn't always involve tears.

The left-hand side of the arc can get pretty messy, and there are things that help and things that hinder the process of moving through the cycle.

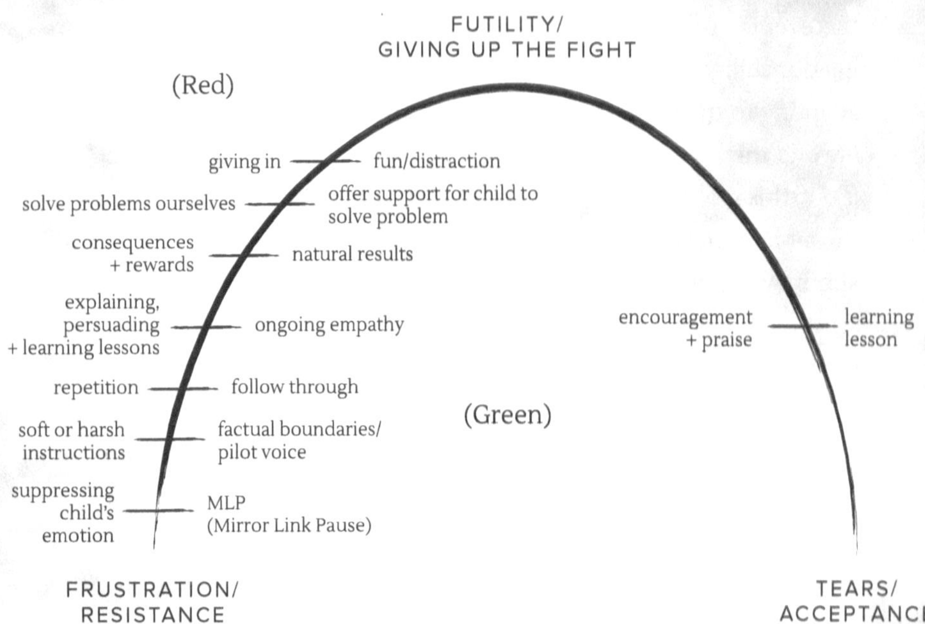

GREEN-BRAIN THINGS THAT HELP	RED-BRAIN THINGS THAT HINDER
MLP	Suppressing their emotion
Factual boundaries – using our pilot voice (explanation to follow)	Soft instructions or harsh instructions
Following through	Repetition
Ongoing empathy	Explaining, persuading or adding a learning lesson
Natural results	Consequences/punishments/rewards
Supporting the child to solve their own problem	Solving the problem ourselves
Fun and distraction	Giving in
Encouragement and praise	Learning lesson

In each case the colour of our brain is the key. Our children can pick up on our brain state no matter how well we think we're hiding it. Any responses in green will be more effective than those in red.

I'm going to go through each of these responses in a bit more detail, but it's important to know you don't need to learn or unlearn all of them. As you read, just notice which of the green ones jump out at you. Also notice which of the red ones you're using a lot and maybe you could consider replacing if they're not working too well. I'll work through them in alternate order, as a lot of the red and green-brain options directly oppose one another and seeing them in contrast can be helpful.

MIRROR, LINK, PAUSE (GREEN BRAIN)

You know the MLP technique already, and it's still the best place to start. You can use it during a boundary-setting situation, especially if a child is hurting another child and you need to jump in. It's much more effective to say "I can see you're really frustrated..." while holding an angry child so they don't hurt anyone, rather than "No hitting!", which functions here as an instructional attempt at a boundary. You may need to slip in a brief ALL for yourself to do this successfully and authentically.

SUPPRESSING THEIR EMOTION (RED BRAIN)

Suppressing their emotion is the opposite of MLP and generally extends the process, as it adds more cortisol to the child's system. "Oh, for goodness sake!" "Someone has to lose!" "You're fine!" "You went first yesterday!" "It's just a cupcake!" are just a few examples of how we aggravate the situation and delay getting to the top of the arc.

FACTUAL BOUNDARIES, USING OUR PILOT VOICE (GREEN BRAIN)

There's a certain tone of voice that is absolutely key to changing the way we set boundaries. It sounds factual, not commanding, nor pleading. It sounds like calm definiteness which, if you remember, is one of the ways I described healthy anger in Chapter Three. Again, the pilot metaphor is a useful one here. Imagine if the pilot of the plane sounded either frustrated or despairing; you'd never want to fly that airline again. You want to know that the pilot is in control. They are calm and reassuring while sharing the facts. Remember, our boundaries are there to give our children safety, so it makes sense that they're less effective if they're emotionally loaded.

A factual voice takes practice, and the tone sounds slightly different for everyone, but it does sound like the behaviour we're after is a given. As a result, there's also more room for support. For example:

"It's time to..."

"Given that you are/we are/it's bedtime..."

"Come and put your shoes away, thank you."

"That's too rough for me/her; off you go. You can come back as soon as you're ready though."

".... Because I've asked you to."

"Try again."

"Follow your trail."

"The answer's not changing (boundary) but let me know if you need help to get through it (support)."

SOFT OR HARSH INSTRUCTIONS (RED BRAIN)

Our boundaries are not requests, so, "Please" or "Can you" aren't all that honest or helpful, unless you're happy to have "No, thank you" as your answer. Once your pilot voice is working well, you may be able to reintroduce these words again but, in the initial stages of changing our tone, they're not definite enough.

I often use "Can you..." again, now that my children have got the message that what I'm asking will be happening. My middle child loves responding with, "I don't know Mum, can I?" It makes us both laugh every time, but only because we both know she's going to.

Negative instructions have a particularly disempowering effect on our ability to get our children to do what we say, "Would you please not", sounds nothing like the pilot, and generally doesn't get much response from our children as a result.

At the other extreme, harsh instructions or orders also come from a red brain and lead straight to red brain for everyone. They may get the job done temporarily, but they function as a disconnection, so a reconnection needs to happen afterwards. When we deliver boundaries in anger, it's also disempowering in the long run, as children slowly become aware that we're not really in charge if we need anger to get things done. Some kids move to flight, meaning they comply but without connection, and others will move to fight and resist.

FOLLOW THROUGH (GREEN BRAIN)

Although it feels as if it would be impossible to follow through with every little thing we ask our kids to do, initially we need to say less and mean all of it. Even with the little things. We often ask our children to do something and then walk away, and then get increasingly cross as we return to find it hasn't been done. Our children need to hear a voice that means what it says. On the other side of this too, as we see our children begin to respond, it helps us grow in confidence.

Start with choosing a few instructions you can follow through with and see if you can stay in green until they're done. You may have to get them to come and do whatever it is, or intervene to stop them doing whatever it is. You may even have to gently lift their chin, look them in the eye and say, "Did you hear me?" just to make sure. It doesn't take them long to start to recognise that this definite, but still very green tone, means business.

"Come and hang your towel up," or "Pop your plate in the dishwasher," or "Put your shoes away," means you stay by the towel, the dishwasher or the shoe rack until it's done. You may even need to go and get your child, and not take care of any of the other things you want to with your own day until it's done. It sounds almost ridiculous and unnecessary – surely they should just do as they're told when they're asked? – but the reality is we're often moving at such speed that our children hear lots of requests or instructions and ignore them, especially when none of it is followed up in green brain.

The end result is we then end up in red brain which sounds like, "This room is a tip, I've asked you a thousand times to clean it up," or "Right, you didn't do as I asked, you've lost your screen-time today," which are far less effective than a simple follow-through. The time it takes to establish the green-brain follow-through is well worth it, as our children learn that when we speak we generally mean it, and that ultimately saves so much time later.

REPETITION (RED BRAIN)

This is pretty much the opposite of the green-brain follow-through. "I've told you a thousand times," doesn't sound like a pilot and, if anything, just highlights how ineffective our earlier attempts or requests have been. Ironically, repetition and hyperbole make a child feel less safe and less likely to do anything we ask. We can't avoid repetition entirely, but if you can follow through whenever possible, repetition is less and less likely to happen.

If you speak and your child doesn't respond, it's your responsibility to make sure they do, not theirs. They soon will respond if the last ten times you made sure it happened. They get used to it.

A lot of parents I work with want respect. I was the same. Unfortunately, wanting respect says more about our own story than our children's. Many of us have grown up with the myth that children should respect their parents and elders, but respect is a spontaneous response. If it's a requirement, it's just another name for fear. 'Respect', from Latin, literally means to 'look again at', similar to when you notice someone you admire. You look twice. It's often a spontaneous reaction to someone or something we notice. It has nothing to do with compliance. Respect is always earned and never expected.

To gain what we call respect, we stay green and make sure they notice that we've said something. Over time, our children grow natural respect for the way we live our lives, as well as just listening to our instructions.

ONGOING EMPATHY, NOT SPECIFICALLY MLP (GREEN BRAIN)

Coming back to empathy during the process, if things get sticky, gives our kids a much more effective message than explanations do. "It is hard to put your clothes away at the end of the day" helps them know you're not changing your mind. Conversely, an explanation like, "If you put your clothes away you'll be able to find them tomorrow" offers lots of room for a retort, like "I can find them on the floor easily" – no matter how green-brained and well-meaning your delivery of the explanation was.

"It's so hard not hitting when you're angry" works better than "We don't hit in our home". We undermine our own authority when we say something can't happen that just has. Not to mention the fact that our kids never say, "Thanks, Dad, I had no idea we weren't supposed to hit". They're in red brain from whatever the initial incident was, as well as because of the boundary we're putting in place. Our goal is to move the whole situation towards green, as no learning happens in red anyway.

EXPLAINING, PERSUADING OR ADDING A LEARNING LESSON (RED BRAIN)

Our children don't have to agree with us. They don't have to like the boundary or even understand why the boundary is as it is, so explaining and persuading aren't generally helpful. Of course, if they're genuinely asking the why? question, you can let them know, "We won't let you go because you're underage and for us that's important." Or if they haven't worked out the consequence ahead, for example, "We'll be late if you hop the whole way," then an explanation can be helpful.

But once they're heading up the arc of their emotional resistance, explanations play into the hands of, and feed the arguments of, your young lawyer – if you have one. Attempting to explain something clearly can also be frustrating for us if we really believe a decently articulated explanation should prevent tricky behaviours from erupting.

Learning lessons can be a contentious area for parents. We're here to pass on wisdom to our children when it's helpful. But learning lessons are almost always unhelpful during conflict. When a child is activated and in the process of navigating the frustration-futility-tears process, they don't have access to the part of their brain that learns – the prefrontal cortex. Our explanations, in those moments, are generally useless.

Parents often ask me when they can offer the learning lesson, or how soon after a problematic incident. I understand the intention, but, personally, I still believe less is more. Rarely does a child find information on why they shouldn't hit or hurt helpful, or find information about why underage drinking or too much screen time will negatively affect their brain compelling. These explanations don't commonly change behaviour next time around.

When all the emotion from the event has died down, it can be helpful to check in with a child to see if they understand what the problem was. The key here is that these conversations are best had after enough time has passed for the cortisol to be low in their and our blood streams. And if your child lets you know they don't want to talk about it, you're better to give them the benefit of the doubt, and leave them alone. If they do seem unsure what all the fuss was about, and open to a conversation, then let them know your thoughts and be open to their input.

This is not about becoming soft or permissive as parents; it's the complete opposite. Connection, not advice, is the quickest route to a child that can manage their raging emotions, cope well with disappointment and make good choices in their lives.

In case you think I'm suggesting we shouldn't impart wisdom or knowledge to our children, I'm really not. Conversations in which we teach our children how the world works are of course part of our parenting journey. It's simply that they're far more effective when we're not attempting to change a specific situation or behaviour. As part of normal family life, when our children are relaxed and in good green-brain connection with us, that's when their brains are in the prime learning state (green) and they much more easily absorb any helpful knowledge and wisdom that we have.

NATURAL RESULTS (GREEN BRAIN)

Giving consequences to our children is a massively over-used parenting strategy, and I want to help untangle it a little here.

Anything that comes with a consequence attached undermines the pilot voice. When we say, "If you don't... I will...," we automatically sound like the boundary isn't a fact and we're not in charge. If the pilot says,"If you don't put your seatbelt on, I'll come and take away your dinner tray," you're likely to wonder what's wrong with the pilot. If, however, they say,

"One of the cabin crew will be coming through to check your seatbelts," you feel fine and know it's going to happen, even if you're not keen.

This type of natural result is very similar to a follow through, but other natural results are created by life itself. These are not created consequences, such as time out, or unrelated punishments. They require a bit of courage on our part, but they often replace what can feel like frustrating and exhausting parenting.

The best example of this that I have is in the morning, one of the most dreaded times of the parenting day (only just beaten by bedtime).

As I've mentioned, a few years ago our mornings were awful. I would wake up every day already anxious about the repeatedly ignored instructions, the arguing, and the meltdowns that were likely to occur before we got out of the house. My pilot voice was beginning to work at other times of the day, but, with the deluge of instructions I issued in the mornings, I wasn't able to follow through. Repetition and rising frustration were my norm. I started working with the idea of natural consequences, which I've since renamed 'natural results', as even the word 'consequences' has become synonymous with 'punishments'.

I looked at what the children needed to do, and which of those tasks had a natural result that affected them and which didn't. Getting dressed, doing their hair, packing what they needed for the day, eating breakfast and making their lunch were the ones with natural results: they would be going to school in their pyjamas, looking a bit of a mess, missing out on activities that they weren't prepared for, and being hungry at school. Making their beds was the only one without a natural result that they would care about, so I dropped that job off the list.

We had a meeting in which I explained I wasn't going to nag them anymore, as none of us were enjoying it. I let them know (in green) that I knew they were quite capable of getting themselves ready, and I was just getting in the way. I said my job was to wake them, make sure there was food for breakfast and for lunches, make lunch for the younger two, and leave the house with all of them with me; the rest was up to them. I also let them know I'd happily take them however ready they were – you have to mean this part to say it, as you may have to follow through – and that I'd give them a few time reminders if it looked like they'd got distracted. None of it was said in a warning tone, and throughout all of it I was genuinely owning my responsibility for having approached our mornings really unhelpfully for everyone, including myself.

It has been one of the most significant changes in our home. The kids loved it and so did I. The beds didn't get made, but that was a small price to pay for doing nothing in the mornings except getting myself ready and watching them mostly just get on with it. If they didn't eat breakfast, I said nothing. If they didn't do their hair, I said nothing. If they didn't get dressed, I said nothing. I did offer little reminders like, "We'll be going in about ten minutes... Are you sure you don't mind being hungry at school? Are you sure you're happy to go in your pyjamas?" But that was all.

They worked out for themselves why they get dressed and why they eat; sometimes they found out the hard way. They got hungry by morning tea because they hadn't had breakfast. They didn't love looking a mess at school or rushing, half-dressed, out of the door. It only happened a few times and they got used to what they needed to do to avoid these scenarios.

Sometimes there were mishaps and they ran out of time to make lunch, or they forgot things they needed. What intrigued me was that they started to apologise for forgetting, and asking if I could wait while they grabbed a sandwich, or could we go back "Because I've forgotten my swim things." Sometimes we could and sometimes we couldn't, but their language had changed, and I could tell they were beginning to take responsibility for their own morning routine, because I let the natural results take their course.

So many of my clients have transformed their mornings the same way. I always recommend having a bag of clothes or uniform in the car and a snack, just so you really will follow through with leaving the house whatever state they're in. Only two of my clients have had to go that far, and left the house carrying struggling children still in pyjamas. You can do this in green, although it's best not to physically touch your children if you're in red brain – outside of emergencies. One of my clients has needed to go through with the natural result once, and one of them twice, and then never again. Even the backup of a separate set of school uniform is a small price to pay for regaining your mornings.

The end of the story is that I now have my pilot voice working much better, so despite there being no natural result, most days even the beds get made.

Here are just a few examples of other natural results. Notice how there's a subtle difference to imposed consequences:

"If you can't play with your sister without hurting her, then you can't play with her until you can." They can choose for how long they need to be at least at arm's length, and then they can have another try.

"If you can't stop throwing food, we'll pop the food away until you can."

"Given that time's up and the TV's going off, are you going to do it, or shall I?"

"Given that you now carry your backpack, if you don't, then it will stay here."

"If you can't stop fighting, I'll just pull over in the car, as I can't drive safely while you are." Try this one when you're not in a rush. You might even get a book out. Their impatience will generally get the better of them and the fight will end.

"If you can't treat your siblings well when you have friends to play, you can't have friends over until you can. Have another go at including your sister/brother."

"As I've said, no more asking, if you ask again, I won't be listening. If you want to talk about anything else, I'm all yours."

"If you take a while to get ready for bed, there won't be time for books."

"If you keep coming out once we've put you to bed, I will keep putting you back." This one can last a while, but I've found it eventually works with most children. You may have to set aside a week or two, and be prepared to follow through with a boring return to bed, over and over, whilst staying in green. It often ends the habit much quicker than frustration and consequences, or giving in and staying with them until they're asleep.

"If you can't get home by the time we've said, you will need to stay in for one invite and then you'll have another chance." This one is closer to a traditional consequence but it's a natural result of our rule that freedom and responsibility go together. It's worked for our teenagers so far, and we've only had to enforce it once.

Mindful boundary-setting means paying attention with kindness as we set our boundaries. All of these boundaries can be said in green. They all keep our connection solid instead of disintegrating into disconnection. Although you may find them hard at first, keep practicing and soon they'll flow. The shift you should feel is that they sound factual, rather than punitive or manipulative.

CONSEQUENCES AND REWARDS (RED BRAIN)

I've already explained a better alternative to either consequences or rewards, but I thought I would add here just a little brain science to reinforce why neither of these work well over the long-term.

Consequences modify a child's behaviour by threatening them with something redder than their current red situation. We do this by removing things they find precious: if we were to leave them in time out, for example, we'd remove their freedom and our presence. They work in the short-term for some children, but only because they're just choosing the lesser of two red options. The drawback is that they don't move into their learning brain while it's happening.

I used to be consequence queen. I had my list of the things I would remove one-by-one, until my children did what I asked. It always worked once the threat had been sufficiently ramped up. What I found baffling, though, was that I would get frustrated, take away things they cared about, and get the compliant behaviour I wanted – only to find them re-peating the same tricky behaviours the next day. It made no sense, until I understood that they hadn't learned anything. They'd just responded in fight mode for a while, until I pushed them so hard that they went into flight mode and gave in.

Rewards do the same but in the opposite direction. They offer exter-nal incentives for good behaviour, which sounds like it might be a good idea, but they don't tend to sustain children for long. Generally, our chil-dren either stop responding to the reward, or they require more elabo-rate ones to keep going. Even if we do get the behaviours we want for a while, rewards (and imposed consequences) encourage an external rath-er than an internal locus of control. Our children soon look to others to either tell them off or affirm them, which often carries on into adulthood. Neither rewards nor consequences create good self-esteem, resilience, or a strong sense of internal identity.

Both consequences and rewards also prevent a child completing the adaptive brain cycle, as they never get to the real 'giving up the fight' part themselves, nor the relief or acceptance that comes with that. They get fast-tracked across to the other side, and don't do the difficult but crucial growth of accepting things they don't like.

KEEP THE PROBLEM WITH THE CHILD, BUT OFFER SUPPORT IF APPROPRIATE (GREEN BRAIN)

Support can be offered anytime during the rise from frustration to futility. It prevents us leaving green and going straight into orange brain and trying to fix the situation. It also reduces conflict long-term, since a child's own solution is much easier for them to repeat. It's a vote of confidence in them and their ability to deal with something or influence an outcome. After all, only they know how a 15-year-old boy solves a 15-year-old boy's problem.

Offering support for them to problem-solve can be part of the pause at the end of MLP, or it can be used anytime. It might look and sound something like this:

"Given that ... is/isn't happening, do you need help to get through it/work it out?"

"You're so good at solving problems. What do you think would help?"

"It doesn't sound like it's working. I'm happy to help you work it out if you need me."

"The answer's not changing, but let me know if you need help to get through it."

"Given that you can't go/do ... – or you have to go/do ... – is there anything that would help?"

"Have you got any ideas? Your ideas are usually better than mine."

"I really don't know how to solve this one. What do you think?"

"What have you tried that's worked before?"

"I'm right here if you need a cuddle, just let me know."

SOLVING (RED BRAIN)

We've looked at this idea already, but consistently solving problems for our children delays their ability to feel the joy of working things out for themselves. It keeps them dependent on us for longer than is helpful and extends our job as parents.

FUN AND DISTRACTION (GREEN BRAIN)

Fun and distraction do wonders for our connection with our children. They bypass the resilience cycle, and aren't consistent enough to rely on, but, if a piggyback or an "Ooh look at that butterfly!" moves your child on from a refusal or an argument, then go for it.

GIVING IN (RED BRAIN)

It's so tempting to give in, when our child is really putting up a fight or getting upset about a boundary we're trying to put in place – whether that be finishing their dinner before dessert, staying in bed or leaving the chocolate alone at the check-out. But imagine the scenario in our earlier metaphor. What if an upset passenger was able to waltz up to the cockpit, throw a tantrum, and get the pilot to change course? The results would be carnage! This is far too much power for our children to have, and ultimately leaves them feeling less safe, even if it makes them happy in the moment.

TOP OF THE ARC AND DOWN THE OTHER SIDE

If you use any or all of the green-brain strategies as your child is rising up the arc, using all the kindness you can muster, you will often see a subtle shift as they hit the top of the arc. You'll notice their shoulders relax a bit. You may see some of the fight go out of them. Their eyes may soften and their muscles start to let go of some of their tension. Often their resistance may take on a different tone.

When they're little, our children will often fall into our arms weeping as they reach this stage and give in. It can be hard to transition from being the cause of the drama to the comforter, but if you've stayed in green brain, it's easier to be there for them. When they're older they may stop protesting, they may just start to do whatever it is we've said, they may disappear for a while to lick their wounds.

As they're coming down to acceptance at the bottom of the arc there's still one way we can jeopardise the process and one way we can enrich it.

LEARNING LESSON (RED BRAIN)

As we've looked at before, you may be tempted to use the moment your child has begun to stop fighting to offer a learning lesson, and explain why they couldn't do what they wanted, or why they have to do what they don't want to do.

Your child has done the hard work of getting through the cycle; they don't need to get their heads around anything else that requires more work at that moment. Not to mention the fact that they're not yet back in their learning brain anyway. Offering a lesson can undo all the good work. If you really feel they may have not understood something about the boundary, you can explain much later when it's all well and truly over.

ENCOURAGEMENT OR PRAISE AFTERWARDS (GREEN BRAIN)

You may not be explicitly teaching them a lesson, but there is a great opportunity here to encourage your child. This is one of my favourite things to do, although I don't do it too often, as it would lose its impact. I gently get down to their eye level and say something like, "You were so cross and now look at you, that's hard to do." Or, "Getting through a disappointment like that is one of the hardest things you'll ever do, I'm so proud of you. That's harder than any race you'll ever win or exam you'll pass. Some adults I know don't even know how to do that yet," or "It's something I'm still learning myself."

Not only is it a lovely way to remind your child that there's no disconnection despite the drama, but it also helps them feel less afraid of their big feelings. They know they're able to process their emotions rather than getting hijacked by them. And you are still teaching them something; you're teaching them that they are emotionally resilient.

If we can stick to the green side of the adaptive brain cycle, over time we tend to see our children's resistance to things they don't want to do, or frustration about things they want to do growing less and less intense. They discover that the outcome rarely changes, and their brain gets skilled at adapting or giving up the fight more quickly.

In my counselling practice I see that children brought up with boundaries set in green – and with empathy accompanying them – require less and less discipline. I've not used the 'discipline' word here so far – it's so often misinterpreted – but it's fitting in the mindful boundaries context as meaning 'to instruct and teach'. When we set boundaries in green, our children's brains really do learn as they go along, and they need less instruction and training from us.

EMPATHY AND BOUNDARIES REQUIRE PRACTICE

The combination of empathy and mindful boundaries is not a simple solution to conflict. They both require persistence and practice. And while they are intuitive, they are not necessarily instinctive. Any response that is somewhat greener than before is a win in my book; with mindful parenting we're really not heading for some kind of perfection. Over time we start to feel that our children do grow and develop before our eyes in all the ways described in Chapter Four, but it is incremental. We need our own mindful practice and our own emotion processing skills to support our parenting when conflict happens. We also need to be both patient and kind with ourselves as we develop these new skills.

6. Thoughts become things

*As a single footstep will not make a path on the earth,
so a single thought will not make a pathway in the mind.
To make a deep physical path, we walk again and again.
To make a deep mental path, we must think over and
over the kind of thoughts we wish to dominate our lives.*

~ Henry David Thoreau

*The greatest weapon against stress is our ability to
choose one thought over another.*

~ William James

Our thoughts and our emotions determine the colour of our brain state far more than the circumstances or the events of our lives do. In Chapter Three, we looked at our emotions: what they are, why they matter and how to work with them. In this chapter, we're looking at our thoughts: how we become aware of what we're thinking, and how we can change our thoughts if they're unhelpful. We're back to exploring the box a little further, fortifying the secure base we offer our children, so they grow up in an increasingly green-brain environment.

Emotions are motions of energy, so once we have an emotion, we can't un-have it. We have to find a way to process it. Our thoughts are a little different. They start out as ideas, and if we spend no time with them, they evaporate into hot air. If we invest time and energy in them, they turn into thoughts, which over time become thought patterns. We have many ideas or possible thoughts every day, some of which become actual thoughts and some of which disappear.

Once we spend a little time thinking a thought, it becomes a tiny piece of protein in the brain – an actual piece of neural pathway. Thoughts really do become things. Over time, repeated thoughts become strong neural pathways in our brain.

For me, ideas are like having a passing acquaintance with someone; thoughts develop from ideas in the same way we would spend more time making friends with someone; and thought patterns are like those familiar relationships that, over time, become part of the fabric of our lives.

Because our brain is – at least partially – made up of the many thoughts we've spent time thinking during our lives, what we think and how we think is crucial to our wellbeing.

VELCRO AND TEFLON

Our brains are wired to look for threats and rewards, but threats take precedence in order to keep us safe. This is just the way we've evolved.

There's no point thinking about how well the crops are growing if there's a tiger on the prowl that needs our attention.

Psychologist Rick Hanson describes this bias as the Velcro/Teflon effect. [1] Our stressful thoughts are like Velcro and they stick, whereas our rewarding thoughts are like Teflon, so they slide. It sounds perverse in a way, but it makes perfect sense when you consider that peaceful or positive thoughts should be our norm. Those thoughts don't need to stick, as they'll be replaced soon enough by more rewarding thoughts. Stressful thoughts, on the other hand, should be genuine signals of danger and therefore much less common; they need to be paid attention to and resolved, so that we can return to safety again.

It's a system that has distinct disadvantages in our lives as we live them today, because we often perceive multiple and ongoing threats that tip us into living day-to-day in an orange-brain state. Many of us are busy fixing and solving all the Velcro thoughts dominating our minds, or even tipping over into living in red brain as we feel overwhelmed by the barrage of stress.

WIRED TO REPEAT

There's a double whammy here too, which is that not only are our brains wired to check for threat first, but they're also wired for repetition. The brain loves repetition, because anything we repeat saves us energy, regardless of whether what we're repeating is working well for us or not. Earlier I talked about the brain schemata – this is where taking the easy, familiar path through a well-built brain structure is natural, as it takes the least energy.

As we think our stressful thoughts, that neural pathway grows, making it then the most accessible thought next time a similar situation arises. It could be our finances, our children's behaviour, or our untidy home that triggers us into an unhelpful, well-worn pathway, regardless of the fact that the situation might more usefully be thought about in a new way. It's a simple but sometimes devastating system.

COGNITIVE BEHAVIOURAL THERAPY

One of the most important and well-researched models in psychology is called Cognitive Behavioural Therapy, or CBT. It's a helpful model for understanding how our thoughts are the driving force behind much of what we do or what happens to us in the rest of our lives.

The Cognitive Behavioural cascade

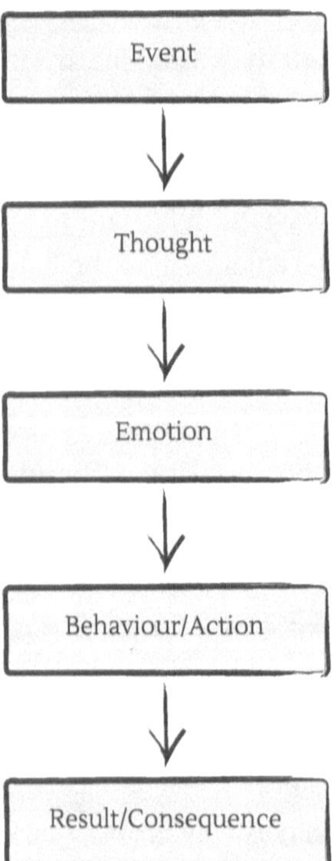

The premise of CBT is that an event leads to a thought, which leads to an emotion, which leads to a behaviour or action, and then this leads to a result or consequence.

Let's look at an example:

EVENT: You're at home, minding your own business or getting on with jobs, and you hear your children start to argue about something.

THOUGHT: *Here we go again.*

EMOTION: Frustration, annoyance, anxiety, resignation, feeling responsible.

BEHAVIOUR: Yell at them; ignore and avoid; zoom in to sort it out.

RESULT: It gets worse.

Let's look at the same example with a different thought:

EVENT: You're at home, minding your own business or getting on with jobs, and you hear your children start to argue about something.

THOUGHT: *I wonder if they'll sort it out.* Or *Kids argue; it's really normal.*

EMOTION: Calm.

BEHAVIOUR: Carry on with what you're doing, and listen just to make sure everyone's safe.

RESULT: They work it out for themselves or, if you do need to intervene, you're in green brain when you do (and you've got MLP up your sleeve to start you off).

Same event, but a different first thought leads to a very different cascade effect.

OUR THOUGHTS ARE KEY

Events are not the defining feature of how our lives turn out. It's our thoughts – specifically how we interpret or perceive events – that makes all the difference. In one sense it's a relief, given we have so little control over what happens in our lives. This includes having not much control over our children, which is something most of you will have probably noticed by now.

Becoming skilful at recognising and changing our thoughts is as helpful to mindful parenting as regulating our emotions.

It's worth mentioning here that we could technically interrupt the cascade with our ALL technique from Chapter Three when we are at the emotion stage of the process. However, the cascade often happens fast, before we realise that frustration or anxiety is filling up our balloon. It might even feel as if the result is an inevitable consequence of the initial event.

I often work with clients who are hoping to change either their own behaviour (stage four of the cascade) or the result (stage five of the cascade), which is usually their child's behaviour. The speed with which these events take place, however, means it's much harder to interrupt the process and behave differently ourselves this far down the cascade, and impossible if changing another person is our hope.

Changing how we think is a much more strategic approach, because it means the cascade itself kicks off less often, saving so many moments – or hours – of disconnection with our children.

CONSCIOUS AND SUBCONSCIOUS THINKING

In order to change our automatic stressful thoughts, we first need to understand what they are and where they come from. Just like our emotions, our thoughts are not random. Our thoughts make perfect sense given the environment we grew up in, our personality and the events that have happened in our lives.

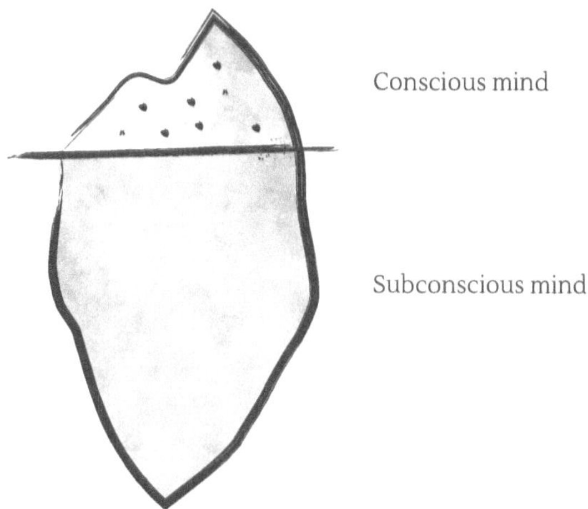

Our mind consists of two parts – our conscious and subconscious. The conscious part is the much smaller part, like the tip of the iceberg. In our conscious mind are the thoughts we're aware of on a day–to-day basis. These are the dots at the top.

Examples of stressful thoughts might be:

- *I don't have enough time.*
- *My kids should listen to me.*
- *The house is a tip.*
- *… kids are better behaved than mine.*
- *We don't have enough money.*
- *There's too much to do.*
- *I need to do better.*
- *He/She doesn't care.*
- *Roll on bedtime!*
- *They know all my buttons.*
- *I just need a break.*

All these thoughts make perfect sense on occasion, but when they become repetitive it means they're connected to deeper thoughts or beliefs that sit further down in the layers of our subconscious. At the very bottom of our subconscious are our deepest thoughts, which are often called our core beliefs.

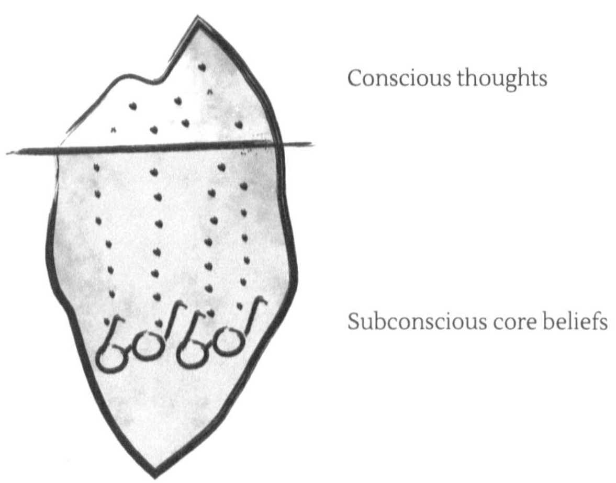

Our core beliefs are formed in childhood. We often don't know much about them, as they're in our subconscious and are more difficult to access than our conscious thoughts. Despite being hidden, they have a significant impact on us because they underpin our day-to-day thinking. They're generally black and white, judgmental and childish by nature. They become like lenses that we're wearing. We see our lives through them, they feel completely true, and we're convinced we're seeing reality accurately.

Here are some examples of common core beliefs, with possible scenarios from our homes of origin. Please bear in mind that these are rough guides only.

- *I'm not good enough* – a high achieving home.
- *I have to get it right/I can't make mistakes* – a home with lots of rules.
- *I'm not important* – a busy home.
- *I need to be in control* – a controlling home, or, sometimes, a chaotic home.
- *I'm responsible* – a home where you had to grow up too fast, or, sometimes, simply as the result of being the eldest child.
- *It's my fault* – a home with a lot of tension.
- *I should.../I shouldn't...* – a judgmental or critical home.

These thoughts are rarely true in terms of what our parents thought of us, and never true in terms of who we are, but they have a childish logic to them. We carry them into adulthood because we automate these perceptions of ourselves when we're very young, and the subconscious repetition of them turns them into our default core beliefs.

Early on in my parenting I became aware that, when my kids didn't listen to me, I had a really intense reaction. I became about five years old again (which is always a clue to a core belief) and I either yelled or I sulked. I would trot out accusations like "that's SO disrespectful!" or deliver loud ultimatums, "When I speak you WILL listen to me." At other times I would cry with despair. It didn't matter; these reactions made them ignore me even more.

I had no idea how to recognise my thoughts or my emotions; I was just fixated on my children's behaviour. I ramped up the consequences until I eventually got them to listen and do what I asked. But the chaos of the process was exhausting, and the cycle continued for years.

I did sometimes wonder about my reaction to not being listened to, because my partner was rarely triggered in the same situations. He generally approached them calmly, as a problem to be solved, and got much better listening, as a result, than I did. Annoying, but also useful when I was utterly hijacked.

When I learnt about core beliefs, some things fell into place for me. I discovered that one of my core beliefs was, *I'm not important* and *My opinions aren't important*, which were beliefs I had developed as a result of my childhood. I got very upset when my children confirmed I wasn't important by not listening to me.

These core beliefs were not how my parents saw me at all, but they do make perfect sense given the type of childhood I had. My partner's core beliefs are different. Not being listened to isn't as much of a trigger for him and didn't cause the cascade effect that it did for me. Understanding has a deeply calming effect on us, even before any kind of transformation takes place. For me, recognising there was logic in our different responses – and that I wasn't just a terrible parent – offered me a way to mindfully pay attention with kindness to myself as the first step towards change.

SELF-FULFILLING PROPHECIES

As you can see from my story, our core beliefs often become self-fulfilling prophecies.

When I believe my voice doesn't matter, I get triggered into helpless or dominating behaviours. These, in the end, make me feel weak rather than strong, my children listen to me less and my 'I'm not important' belief gets a bit more evidence to prove it's true.

If, for example, my core belief is, *I'm not much fun* or *I don't make friends easily*, then in social situations I'm likely to be either nervous or trying too hard. Both behaviours are likely to corroborate my core belief, as others are then much less likely to enjoy my company.

Another thought might be *I don't have enough time* or *There's too much to do*. Although these are common stressful thoughts for parents, they're not core beliefs as they're not childish thoughts. That said, they're likely to be sitting on core beliefs such as *I need to do more, I need to do better* or *I'm not good enough.* Even these conscious thoughts become a self-fulfilling prophecy, as they produce stress, raise our heart rate and tip us into red brain, which means we become much less efficient, creative or productive with our time.

On the other hand, *I have plenty of time* and *I can do all I need to do for today* trigger the green-brain state. We're then much more likely to move through our day present to our surroundings, able to make better choices and, ironically, be more effective and productive.

REPEATING PATTERNS

Core beliefs are also often repeated down the generations. So many clients I see feel despair that they seem to be repeating some of the patterns they grew up with and can't understand why. It's not just bad luck; it's built into the system.

When I'm triggered by not being listened to, I get emotional and dominating — a logical but unhelpful response to feeling unimportant. Then my children don't feel listened to, and it's highly likely some of them will develop the same core belief. None of us intend that our children have the same negative beliefs that we do, but the core belief causes a self-protective reaction that perpetuates itself.

If we believe we can't make mistakes or we can't fail, our children will learn these same things in two powerful ways. Firstly, they'll watch and learn. They'll see our reactions when we break a glass, spill our coffee or burn the dinner, and will naturally develop the belief that those so-called failures should be avoided at all costs. They will also experience our core belief in a more direct form, because with that belief in place we will find our children's very normal failures and mistakes hard to handle. We're likely to criticise them and push them to greater levels of achievement. The cycle continues.

IDENTIFYING OUR NEGATIVE THOUGHT PATTERNS

Before we can change the way we think, we need to explore what we're thinking in both our conscious mind and then deeper in our subconscious. The following insight questions will begin to help you identify some or your thought patterns.

INSIGHT QUESTIONS - STRESSFUL THOUGHTS

Write down your three most recurrent stressful thoughts. Make sure you keep them 'raw' - they won't start with *I feel* or *I think.*

1.

2.

3.

Finish each of these sentences with the first thing that comes to your mind. Try not to think too hard about your answers.

I am...

Others are...

The world is...

I have to be... or else...

As a child, what was your role in the family? For example, the funny one, the baby, the peacekeeper, the black sheep, the sporty one, the naughty one, the shy one...

Some of you will find recurrent themes and patterns jump out at you. You might identify clear themes that link to what you know of your childhood and that make perfect sense. Others of you will have hints of a pattern emerging. For others still, it may feel unclear what these patterns are and why. Hopefully you'll be more aware of the stressful thoughts you have on a regular basis, and some of the deeper subconscious thinking underneath, even if the links to your childhood don't yet make much sense.

I'm going to introduce you to a mindful self-enquiry technique, designed by author Byron Katie, that gently guides you through a process by which you start to unhook yourself from either a stressful thought or a core belief. [2] You can choose to start with a day-to-day thought or start a little deeper. Because so many of our conscious thoughts emerge from our subconscious ones, the deeper you go, the more effective the process. If you feel as though you have identified a core belief in the previous exercise, that's a great place to start. The more important criterion, though, is that you find a thought that you would love to change.

CORE SKILL 6: THOUGHT INQUIRY

Write down the stressful thought or negative core belief that you would like to change.

Now follow the questions. It can be helpful to shut your eyes and 'feel' your way into some of your answers. When I do this exercise, I use a red pen to write my answers to questions three and four, and a green pen from then on.

1. Is the thought true? (Yes/No only)

If Yes, go to the next question. If No, skip to question three.

2. Can you be 100% certain it's true? (Yes/No only)

3. How do you feel when you think this thought?

- In your body? Write down what shifts happen in your body when you think this thought.

- In your emotions? Again, write down all the different emotions that the stressful thought or core belief produces.

4. What sorts of things do you find yourself doing when you think this thought?

And what sorts of things are you unable to do, or do you find difficult to do, when you think this thought?

5. Imagine you woke up in the morning and the thought had disappeared. You couldn't access it anywhere; it's gone. Really stretch your imagination here. How do you feel without this thought?

- In your body?

- In your emotions?

What sorts of things do you do, or what do you stop doing, without this thought in your life?

6. Now you've imagined your life without the thought, you need to find a new thought to replace it. What is the opposite of the original thought? This is called the Turnaround. It will likely feel completely untrue, but remember that's only because the original thought has a strong neural pathway connected to it.

Write down your new turnaround thought – the opposite of the original, stressful thought. (Be brave. The opposite of I'm not good enough really is I am good enough!)

7. Now find three pieces of evidence why the new thought is true.

1.

2.

3.

Once the new thought is there and the evidence is in place, you already know that the original thought – although dominant – is not actually true. I often think of this thought inquiry technique as being like a court of law. If there's valid evidence for the defence, there's no guilty verdict. Your evidence to support the opposite thought has already revealed the shadow of doubt.

REPEATING THE NEW THOUGHT

The rest of the process is about pure repetition. We've seen already that our brain pathways grow, not as a result of something being true, but simply because of something being repeated. It's how we learn anything, whether a musical instrument or a language. It's even how we learned to walk. We repeated it – and tried – over and over until it came more naturally. It's the journey of neuroplasticity that I described in Chapter One. Here's a reminder of the way that journey progresses:

STAGE	SKILL LEVEL	OLD PATHWAY	NEW PATHWAY
1	Unaware unskilled	Existing	Not existing
2	Aware unskilled	Dominant	Existing
3	Aware skilled	Existing	Dominant
4	Unaware skilled	Dormant	Existing

When I initially completed my own insight questions, and my own thought inquiry, it was at a stage in my parenting when all five of our children were still young. I was overwhelmed by their different needs, and I really was losing it on an almost daily basis. This is what mine looked like then. Three stressful thoughts:

- *I can't do this.*
- *They should have a different mum.*
- *I can't do this.*

This is technically only two thoughts, but the *I can't* was so strong that it dominated my thinking. When I moved on to the four sentence starters, I came up with this:

- *I am... small and insignificant*
- *Others are... bigger and more important than me*
- *The world is... an amazing place to explore if I had the courage to do so*
- *I have to be... impressive or else I won't be noticed*

My role at home was the rebellious younger child.

As I looked at my answers, I could see a pattern emerging: the core belief of insignificance and the attempt to overcome it by becoming important, adventurous, sometimes rebellious and more impressive than I felt. Many of those strategies had worked for me up to a point, but becoming a parent had launched me back into my actual core beliefs that were hidden underneath, which sounded – at a conscious level – like *I can't do this*.

In my experience of working with parents, it's a common pattern. We hide our negative core beliefs well, until our children blow our cover.

I chose *I am small and insignificant* for my thought inquiry work. As you can see, there's no right or wrong here. I could have chosen *My children need a different mum* or *I can't do this*, and I would still have found significant freedom from turning either of those around. My turnaround thought wasn't an exact opposite, as in *I am large and significant*. That didn't resonate with me, so my turnaround became *I am just the right size*.

My new, healthier thought means so many different things to me now. I've repeated it so often that I truly believe it most of the time. It's not about my physical size, particularly – although I am small, which I used to mind, and now I don't. The bigger picture, for me, is that I am the right size for my life. I am the right mum for my kids, and the right person to write this book and do the work I do. It doesn't mean I'm the best; it means I'm glad to be me and *I can do this*, whatever 'this' happens to be.

It's been a significant transformation, and the wonderful knock-on effect is that my children all happen to be the right size for their lives too. It's not just a reality in my mind; I see the confidence growing in them where they were previously restricted or criticised as a result of my own negative core belief.

It might feel like a huge responsibility that our core beliefs get handed down, but I also see how perfectly designed the parent-child relationship is. Our children really do breathe in our sense of self so, as we develop ours, the difficult part of the work is done, and they just receive it.

Once you've written out your own process, the final step is to get creative with your repetition. Make it part of your daily mindfulness practice; turn it into a screensaver; write it on your mirror; stick post-its up wherever you can (ideally away from the kids – they don't need to know the pilot is still in training). And then make sure you enjoy the changes you start to experience without that thought in your life. And enjoy the deeper connection it enables you to have with your children, which is – after all – the aim of this book.

I often get asked when it's time to tackle a second thought or core belief with the Thought Inquiry process. There's no right answer to that. Some people have a few core beliefs or stressful thoughts in process at the same time, whereas others (like me) focus on one at a time. It partly depends on whether you're working at a conscious or core belief level; the deeper you go, the more impact you have on many of your stressful day-by-day thoughts.

A general rule of thumb is to check in with the colour of your brain. If green is becoming your home base, it really doesn't matter how that's happening. If your daily mindfulness practice and ability to process your emotions is creating a green cushion, then one core belief turnaround may well be enough.

7. Growing your mindful family

It is good to have an end to journey toward;
but it is the journey that matters, in the end.

~ Ernest Hemingway

How we spend our days is, of course,
how we spend our lives.

~ Annie Dillard

Growing a mindful family is a goal I encourage every parent I work with to consider. I also encourage them to attach some specific targets to that goal. The starting point is always to grow your own personal green brain, which has a natural overflow effect on your family. But intentional practices as specific as validating emotions, and as broad as developing a deep connection with each child, will help that overflow.

Setting goals is a key aspect of mindful parenting – despite perhaps seeming to be a contradiction – so it's important to explain the distinction between green- and orange-brain goal-setting. There's an obvious danger in even reading a parenting book, that you might try and become a 'better' parent or have a 'better' family, which can easily trigger the orange, if not red, brain state.

STATE OF FLOW

As I've said before, green is a motivated and productive brain state. It's a growing and developing brain state. Green-brain goal-setting is like adding a destination to an energy that's already in motion. It's not about improving something that's not good enough or fixing something that's faulty. 'Flow' is the name given to this energy. It's a combination of having a very present brain state and holding a clear goal at the same time.

The state of flow doesn't necessarily feel calm, but you feel in control of your stress levels and your brain is fully engaged, often with high energy. It's associated with being fully immersed in something, with focus and enjoyment. The idea of flow has been extensively researched, particularly in the artistic community. However, it's not just for artists; flow can apply to anything you do, from cleaning the house to playing a sport, to connecting with your kids, or engaging in a project at work.

The key difference between the mindful state of flow and setting goals in orange or red is your relationship to the future. If you believe the future will be better than the present, and that you need to achieve things and reach your goals in order to be happy, your brain will lose much of the energy and creativity that you need to get there. With future happiness as your motivation, the journey is generally marked by stress.

In the state of flow, your enjoyment of life isn't tied to your goal. Rather than happiness being the result of achieving your goal, happiness fuels the journey.

In green brain, when you're mindfully immersed in the present moment, all of your brain's resources are available to you. You think outside the box, find creative solutions to problems, see the bigger picture, relate better to others, make more intuitive decisions and even hold the outcome lightly. It's the most productive and efficient brain state in which to head towards any goal you want to set for yourself.

When a goal is reached, the brain triggers the success state that we looked at in Chapter One, giving us an intensive shot of all the green-brain hormones we enjoy so much. When we've taken a green-brain approach to getting there, though, we easily return to our base level. We're not so dependent on success for green-brain health in our lives, as it's already part of our day-to-day existence.

The state of flow is the best brain state for making decisions, setting goals, and for growing a mindful family. Children thrive in a green-brain home where they see clear goals set from time to time, as they become immersed in the flow. They also learn how to set goals for the future without being dissatisfied with the present.

MINDFUL OR MYTHICAL FAMILIES

Before we look at what a mindful family is, and what aspect you might want to set as your first goal, I want to look at what a mindful family is not. Just as goal setting can become confused with improving our lives, so the idea of a mindful family can be confused with the mythical or Facebook family.

It doesn't take much for most of us to conjure up our picture-perfect family. They will all be a little different depending on our personal aspirations, but in my experience of talking with parents, these fantasy families have a lot in common, and often do get confused with the idea of a mindful family.

During every parenting course that I run, we create a list. It inevitably looks something like this:

- Everyone's happy all the time
- The kids are clean and well-dressed
- They're all high achievers in something like sport or academics or music
- There are two parents in the home
- The parents love each other deeply
- The children all get on well with each other
- No one raises their voice
- The house looks like a designer paradise
- The family does lots of stuff outdoors together
- They have hardly any screen time, as they're all busy being creative
- They eat healthy, homemade food, which all the children love
- They have gorgeous holidays, the sun shines every day, and no one fights.

I love this list. It makes me laugh every time. But there is a darker side to this fantasy. While it looks like a bit of fun to pull it together, many of us actually do carry some, or all, of these ideas in our minds, as though this is really what a family should be like. More dangerously, we may even believe that the family down the road is living the dream because the outside appearance or a parade of social media posts suggest it might be the case.

Mindful families don't look like this family. If you cast your mind back to Chapter Three, you may remember that in order to live a healthy, happy life, we need to feel fear, sadness, anger and happiness on a regular basis. So do our children. Without healthy access to all four of these emotions, we lose happiness along the way. Learning to process our emotions well is the journey we're on, not getting rid of the more difficult ones.

If you have a look at the fantasy family list, you'll see only one emotion present – happiness – which means a few things are missing. No sadness means there's no grief or loss or disappointment. Without the emotion of sadness in our families, we don't have deep relationships with anyone. We cheerlead others into suppressing their sadness as a response to life's difficulties, instead of encouraging them to communicate and share their feelings. Imagine sadness in this family and it starts to look a little different.

No fear means no courage. Courage isn't the absence of fear; it's fear in motion. If we're not afraid of anything, we never experience courage. Sometimes we – both parents and children – get stuck in fear and need support for a while before we find our courage. Again, if you add a healthy expression of fear to the fantasy family, the family starts to develop and change even more.

And finally, anger. Even anger is needed in every family. Anger is about individuating and having healthy boundaries for ourselves, as well as fighting against injustice. It may come out explosively, because learning to communicate anger in green brain develops over time. But feeling anger is still a sign of health and needs to be allowed in mindful families. If there's no anger, it means that someone in the family is the autocrat, and that prevents others from being free to express their feelings safely. Add a little healthy anger into the mix and the fantasy family is now starting to look a lot more mindful.

MINDFUL FAMILIES: RETURNING TO NATURAL PARENTING

As long as our children have food, shelter and safety, they only need a solid green-brain connection with us to thrive. Mindful parenting is the most natural expression of parenting there is, and mindful families flow naturally from that. It's not rocket science; it's a perfect design. It's simple too – most definitely not flash – and it's all our children need.

But the reality is that we live increasingly busy and stressful lives. We need to practise mindfulness in order to learn how to be calm and present for our children, as it often doesn't happen naturally anymore. Our children learn and grow by messy trial and error, feel lots of emotions and test our boundaries, but unfortunately many of us have lost the ability to allow that sort of human development to happen under our roofs in the inconvenient and miraculous way it does. Again, we need to re-learn some skills. Finally, as adults, we also bring our own messy and complex childhood stories into our parenting, and we're often unsure how to cushion our own triggers with understanding and kindness, so we need skills and tools to do that.

Mindful parenting is more a process of returning than anything else. It's about learning tools and techniques to help us get back to our natural green-brain state – a state in which we enjoy deep, connected relationships with our children. It's a state that enables our children to grow and develop in an atmosphere of unconditional acceptance and love.

So many of the parents I work with make the observation that the skills they're learning feel intuitive, or that they're really just unearthing skills buried under layers of busyness or stress. The tools themselves may be fresh, but the capabilities they release in us feel more like a restoration of something original rather than the creation of something brand new.

I call it the 'art of subtraction'. Even though it may seem as if we're improving our parenting or our families, the process itself is better described as one in which we're gently and kindly skimming off the extra layers – of reactivity, or expectation, or anxiety, or control – to get down to what's underneath for all of us. What's underneath is simply mindful human connection.

DRAMA TRIANGLES

As the conflict zone is generally the arena that most clearly separates mindful families from other families, one of the most helpful ways I've found to describe how a mindful family works is using the Karpman drama triangle model [1].

In the red corner, we have the persecutor, the victim and the rescuer parent, and in the green corner, we have the assertive, the caring and the self-aware parent.

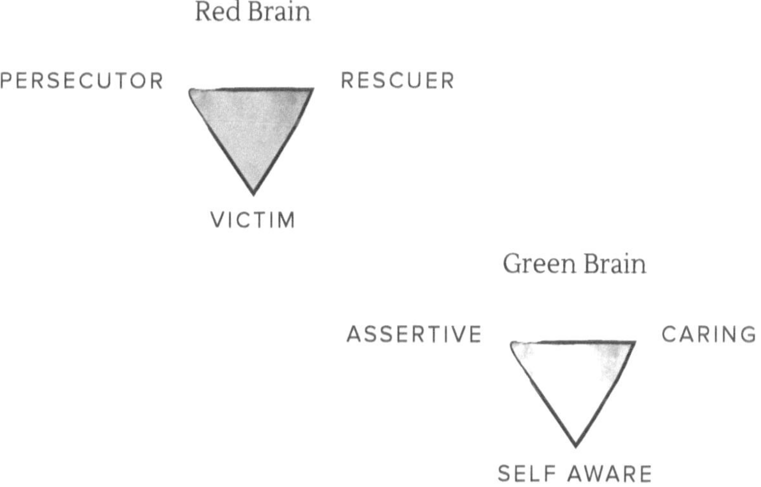

These are all roles we play in response to drama. Although we do all play all these roles, most of us have a bias towards some more than others. We all have favourite roles, if you like.

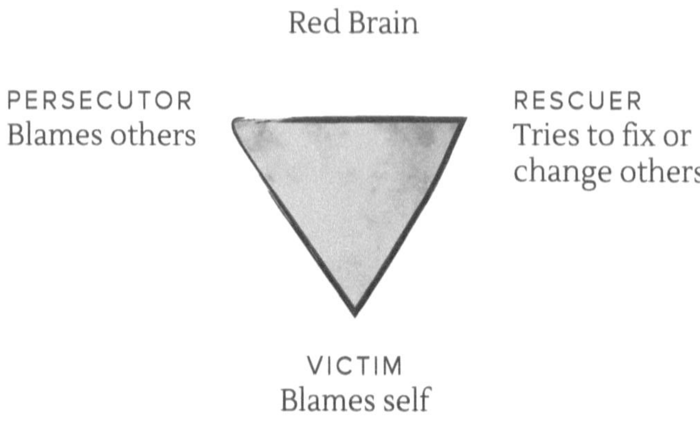

In the red triangle, the persecutor is the classic angry parent. In this mode we may be noisy and yell a lot, or we could be steely and controlling. We're driven by the feeling that we're right and that others are to blame. Cortisol and adrenaline course through the bloodstream during times of conflict, and we're in red-brain fight mode much of the time. The persecutor parent generally feels that the kids are to blame, but it could sometimes be our partner, or even the dog. The point is, it's anyone but ourselves.

Persecutor behaviours tend to be controlling and dominating, possibly aggressive or at least unyielding. They also tend to cause others, especially our children, to either withdraw or retaliate. When we're in persecutor mode, we direct our focus of attention outwards to others and we're not looking inwards much at all.

The victim is the classic helpless parent. In victim mode, we may be self-pitying and weepy or self-critical and harsh. We're driven by the feeling that everything is our fault and we can't do this. We may even question what we've done to deserve this life. Cortisol and adrenaline are also flooding through the victim parent's system, but here the hormones are causing red-brain flight mode. Our kids are generally perceived as the aggressors, but it could sometimes be our partner. It's less often the dog.

Victim behaviours tend to be manipulative and stressful, and cause others – especially our children – to run a mile, walk on eggshells, or try desperately to help. The victim parent's focus of attention is often directed inwards.

The rescuer is the classic fix-it, solve-it parent. In rescuer mode we may start out orange, while the persecutor and victim are automatically red. We may be kind, but also fussy, busy and over-involved in our children's lives. We're driven by the feeling that we're responsible for everything. In parenting it's generally our children we think need our help, but it can also be our partner.

Rescuer behaviours tend to be disempowering, and cause others – especially our children – to either resist help and advice at all costs, or become dependent on us, which often leads to needy and anxious behaviours. Like the persecutor, the rescuer's focus of attention is outward, rather than inward.

MOVEMENT AROUND THE RED-BRAIN TRIANGLE

We all have a natural bias towards one of the three roles, but we also have patterns of movement around the red triangle as well. For example, when our rescuing is unsuccessful, which is much of the time, we might go in either direction. We may dive down to victim, which sounds like "Well, I was only trying to help!", or feels like *Why doesn't anyone appreciate me?* Or we zoom over to persecutor, which sounds like, "Well, if you're not going to accept my help, you can sort out your own problems".

As persecutors, we may get stuck in persecuting and simply ramp up the anger, but we may also dive down to the victim role when we run out of steam – especially if nobody's listening or responding to our threats or consequences. Persecutors make tricky victims: we feel the victimisation more acutely than those who start out as victims, and are more familiar with feeling to blame. Persecutors are less likely to move towards the rescuer role.

Victims are also less likely to move towards rescuer, but easily switch to persecutor. An angry victim parent can be even more devastating than a straightforward persecutor, as we have an additional element of emotional manipulation thrown into the mix. With even less access to the edit button, we say and do things even a persecutor might not.

Each role in the red-brain triangle has a matching one in the green-brain triangle that is a distinctly different version of the same role. The rescuer becomes caring and connected in green brain; the persecutor becomes assertive; and the victim becomes self-aware. Between these green-brain roles, you'll see the six mindful parenting skills are all in active use.

The assertive parent can apply safe and healthy boundaries whilst staying in green. When we're in assertive mode, we make sure our children feel that someone is comfortably in charge, and that they, themselves, don't need to be. The assertive parent is driven by the belief that they are the pilot and that their children are not flying the plane. Unlike in persecutor mode, we stay calmer and more factual. We tend to be able to stick more consistently to the boundaries we set without relying on consequences or rewards to enforce or elicit the behaviours we want.

As a self-aware parent, we will have been cultivating skills behind the scenes, so that during conflict we can turn inwards and pay attention – with kindness – to what we're feeling and thinking. This is in contrast to the victim who turns inward with self-blame.

When we're functioning in self-awareness, we have a deep sense of responsibility for our own green brain. We have a regular mindfulness practice, so we live with lower stress levels and enjoy the present moment more often. We've been practicing ALL (Acknowledge, Link, Let Go), so we have a more accurate sense of our emotional triggers and why they make perfect sense. We may also have begun to work with our stressful thoughts or core beliefs, so we have more protection from the cascade effect that an event may cause. In times of conflict, all these skills become powerful tools for keeping us in green.

As a connected parent, we will have built up a strong bond with each child behind the scenes by paying attention with kindness and curiosity to their lives. When conflict arises, we're able to draw on that healthy connection: we offer empathy and support using MLP (Mirror, Link, Pause), allowing the child's problem-solving capacity to emerge. The posture of the caring parent is of healthy distance, in contrast to the rescuer's over-involved stance, which can involve micro-managing our children.

Internally, as caring parents we feel that our children have all they need to live their own lives well. We believe ourselves to be the gardener, not the sculptor or carpenter. Children of caring, connected parents feel known and validated; they learn to solve their own problems and develop resilience and self-esteem as a natural part of the process of growing up.

In all three green-brain roles, we have some or all the hormones serotonin, oxytocin and dopamine in our system. These hormones keep our muscles relaxed, our heart rate even, our breathing normal, our focus open, and our tone warm and calm.

Movement around the green-brain triangle tends to feel quite natural. If our initial reaction is green, we then generally move between the roles without getting stuck. We may start with self-awareness by taking a few breaths or doing a quick ALL, or we might start with empathy. In some cases, we move straight into boundary-setting but, wherever we start, our brain is in its most creative state, so we can shift direction easily if we need to.

YOUR ROLES AND MOVEMENT IN THE TRIANGLES

We all spend time in both triangles when we're faced with conflict, but we tend to have a bias towards certain roles as well as certain patterns of movement, particularly in the red-brain triangle. It's really helpful to identify your favourite roles and patterns, as well as looking at how your green-brain skills are developing. These are the responses that will ultimately enable you to not only grow a mindful family, but realise you're already part way there.

INSIGHT QUESTIONS - THE DRAMA TRIANGLES

Draw your own red-brain triangle, noting as you go your more dominant role and your patterns of movement around the red triangle.

Draw your green-brain triangle, noting as you do which skills you're beginning to develop. Some you will be developing the ability to use in the moment, and some are investment skills – practices you may be developing on a regular basis outside the conflict zone.

Write down any ways you can see that you're already responding in one or more of the green triangle roles, as opposed to the red roles, during drama or conflict.

So, that's what a mindful family looks like. Mindful families are all about the colour of the parent's brain and especially how we respond in drama or conflict. They're not much about the children at all. Our children's brains absorb the colour of ours like sponges. The investment is ours to make. Slowly, bit-by-bit, as we develop our everyday mindful practice, add techniques that offer us the powerful pause to replace reactivity or trying to fix every challenging scenario, we begin to preserve connection with our children. That's what ultimately transforms our families.

I had a client recently who came to see me after my parenting course with a list of problems with her six-year-old daughter: "She has force-10 tantrums, she kicks and hits us, and then tells us she's the most horrible person in the world". I asked gently about the mum's brain colour and she said, "Totally orange. I'm wired that way".

We spent an hour together going through the green-brain strategies – a short daily mindful practice, a bit more connection with her daughter, ALL for her own emotions and stress, MLP to engage with empathy with her daughter, and some immovable boundaries when needed. She emailed me a few days later to say it was already working. There was no focus on changes to her daughter here, just a gentle focus on the mum.

Mindful parenting doesn't bring about change this quickly every time, and I'm sure this particular mum has had many red-brain days with her daughter since then. But the journey is still the same: focus on the skills, grow the green-brain cushion, develop deep connection with your children, and protect your connection from breaking during conflict as fiercely and gently as you can.

TO SUMMARISE: THE SIX MINDFUL PARENT SKILLS

There are six core skills at the heart of mindful parenting: three are personal, three are directed toward our children.

The personal skills:

1. MINDFUL BREATH AND SENSES

A regular, brief daily practice that develops the life-changing skill of being able to pay attention to the present moment with kindness and curiosity.

2. ACKNOWLEDGE, LINK, LET GO (ALL)

A regular practice of turning inwards towards our emotions to understand why they make sense, and to process them healthily. We can use ALL with our current emotions, but also to process the deeper ones linked to our childhood story.

3. THOUGHT INQUIRY

An occasional practice that helps us recognise our unhealthy, conscious thought patterns and our subconscious negative core beliefs. Thought inquiry is then followed up with regular repetition of the new healthier thought.

The skills directed towards our children:

4. UNCONDITIONAL CONNECTION

A day-by-day relationship in which our children feel our connection, whether we're physically together or not. The connection is fundamentally unconditional, and likely to be the only one in their lives that offers that cushion. It's this connection that enables healthy brain development, and is the greatest common denominator in sustained behavioural change.

5. MIRROR, LINK, PAUSE (MLP)

A regular response we offer our children when they're experiencing a tricky emotion or event. It replaces our frustration, opinions or advice. As we offer them empathy for their emotions, they develop resilience, dignity, self-esteem and problem-solving skills.

6. MINDFUL BOUNDARY-SETTING

A skill we need to practice so that we can apply factual boundaries around our children's unsafe or unsustainable behaviours. Boundaries set in green, and without consequences, are the most powerful way our children learn safe behaviour. The pilot voice, plus the follow through, reduces anxiety in children as well as enabling them to modify their behaviour in the moment.

Now's the time for one last brief exercise, in which you get to set two goals for yourself, to focus on.

GREEN-BRAIN GOAL-SETTING

Circle one skill from each section that you are going to focus your practice on for the next few weeks:

Mindful breath and senses,
Acknowledge, Link, Let Go (ALL)
Thought inquiry

Unconditional connection
Mirror, link, pause (MLP)
Mindful boundary-setting

Now write down how you are going to invest in these two practices. It may be helpful to turn back to the relevant chapters for some ideas. Keep the steps realistic so you don't tip yourself out of green in the process, but stay in the flow as much as possible.

This is your goal-setting exercise – being clear about your next steps.

Once you have repeated these two skills enough that they've become second nature to you, come back to the list and choose your next skill, or skills, to focus on.

A FINAL WORD OF ENCOURAGEMENT

Information on its own doesn't lead to transformation. Reading a book like this won't change anything in your brain or your home. My goal has been to try to create a set of practices that are as kind, gentle, accessible and simple as possible, so you can choose to practice as much or as little as works best for you.

Only practice creates real change. The awareness that keeps me going on even my worst parenting days is that my brain is wired to work in green, so every time I turn myself in that direction it feels like I'm coming home.

Be patient, trust the practices and, above all, enjoy the journey.

Acknowledgements

Thank you, first of all, to Chantal for introducing me to the colours of my brain with such brilliance and such kindness, and for inspiring me to write this book at all.

To Christina at Intelligent Ink for being an editing genius, and for your relentless but gentle encouragement to keep going.

To Dave at Intelligent Ink for going much further than simply polishing the final product, for adding incredible insight, and for ploughing your way with extraordinary commitment through a book about parenting.

To the team at Husk for your beautiful design and for your gorgeous stress-free approach. I think you all have very green brains.

To Keri for your infectious enthusiasm, for telling everyone you meet about Mindful Parenting and for your marketing expertise.

To Martin for making the baffling world of online publishing seem so simple and for steering me through it.

To Pieter for your endless patience with my endless questions, and for getting on with the unseen things that make visible things like this book possible.

To Rach, Prim and Caroline for reading and contributing to my early drafts, and for being inspiring mindful parents yourselves.

To Sarah for every day of friendship and parenting together since that day on the side of the sandpit.

To Lou for reading my very first efforts, for contributing your parenting stories, for your beautiful book design as well as your own beautiful design, and for finding green in me on even my reddest days.

To each and every parent I've worked with and learned so much from, and especially to those who generously allowed me to include their stories in this book – thank you.

And to Simon for patiently watching me slowly catch up to your remarkable green-brain parenting with a little of my own.

References

Chapter 1

1. Giulia M. Dotti Sani and Judith Treas, 'Educational gradients in parents' child-care time across countries 1965-2012', *Journal of Marriage and Family*, April 2016.

2. Tony Crabbe, *Busy: How to Thrive in a World of Too Much Noise*, Grand Central Publishing, 2015.

Chapter 2

1. The American Mindfulness Research Association - www.amra.org

2. Matt Killingsworth, 'Want to be happier? Stay in the moment' [video file], retrieved from https://www.ted.com/talks/matt_killingsworth_want_to_be_happier_stay_in_the_moment?, November 2011.

3. Britta K. Hölzel, James Carmody, Mark Vangel, Christina Congleton, Sita M. Yerramsetti, Tim Gard and Sara W. Lazar, 'Mindfulness practice leads to increases in regional gray matter density', *Psychiatry Research*, January 2011.

Chapter 3

1. Pauline Skeates, Insight International. https://insight-international.org/new-zealand

Chapter 4

1. Gordon Neufeld, 'Working with Troubled Children', Presentation, Auckland, New Zealand 2015.

2. Gordon Neufeld and Gabor Maté, *Hold On To Your Kids*, Ballantine Books, 2006.

3. Shefali Tsabary, https://drshefali.com

4. Gordon Neufeld and Gabor Maté, *Hold On To Your Kids*, Ballantine Books, 2006.

Chapter 5

1. Dr Seuss, *Horton Hears a Who!*, Random House, 1954.

2. Gordon Neufeld and Gabor Maté, *Hold On To Your Kids* Ballantine Books, 2006.

Chapter 6

1. Rick Hanson, *Hardwiring Happiness: The Practical Science of Reshaping Your Brain and Your Life*, Rider, 2013.

2. Byron Katie and Stephen Mitchell, *Loving What Is*, Harmony Books, 2002.

Chapter 7

1. Stephen Karpman, 'Fairy tales and script drama analysis', *Transactional Analysis Bulletin*, 1968.

 Shirley Pastiroff is a counsellor, mindfulness trainer and parent coach. She has trained thousands of parents in the techniques described in this book, and now works across the education and commercial sectors as well as with individuals and families. Shirley is a former BBC documentary-maker and lives in Auckland with her husband and five children.